EVERYDAY ECONOMICS

Previous Books by Lawrence H. Officer

*An Econometric Model of Canada under the
Fluctuating Exchange Rate.* Harvard University Press, 1968.

The International Monetary System: Problems and Proposals
(co-editor). Prentice-Hall, 1969.

Canadian Economic Problems and Policies
(co-editor). McGraw-Hill, 1970.

*Supply Relationships in the Canadian Economy:
An Industry Comparison.*
M.S.U. International Business and Economic Studies,
Michigan State University, 1972.

Issues in Canadian Economics
(co-editor). McGraw-Hill Ryerson, 1974.

*The Monetary Approach to the Balance of Payments:
A Survey* (co-author). International Finance Section,
Princeton University, 1978.

So You Have to Write an Economics Term Paper . . .
(co-author). Michigan State University Press, 1981.

Purchasing Power Parity: Theory, Evidence and Relevance.
JAI Press, 1982.

International Economics (editor).
Kluwer-Nijhoff, 1987.

*Between the Dollar-Sterling Gold Points:
Exchange Rates, Parities and Market Behavior, 1791–1931.*
Cambridge University Press, 1996; paperback reissue, 2007.

Monetary Standards and Exchange Rates
(co-editor). Routledge, 1997.

*Pricing Theory, Financing of International Organisations
and Monetary History.* Routledge, 2007.

*Two Centuries of Compensation for U.S. Production Workers
in Manufacturing.* Palgrave Macmillan, 2009.

EVERYDAY ECONOMICS

Honest Answers to Tough Questions

LAWRENCE H. OFFICER

palgrave
macmillan

EVERYDAY ECONOMICS
Copyright © Lawrence H. Officer, 2009
All rights reserved.

First published in 2009 by PALGRAVE MACMILLAN® in the United
States–a division of St. Martin's Press LLC, 175 Fifth Avenue, New York,
NY 10010.

Where this book is distributed in the UK, Europe and the rest of the
world, this is by Palgrave Macmillan, a division of Macmillan Publishers
Limited, registered in England, company number 785998, of Houndmills,
Basingstoke, Hampshire RG21 6XS.

Palgrave Macmillan is the global academic imprint of the above
companies and has companies and representatives throughout the world.

Palgrave® and Macmillan® are registered trademarks in the United States,
the United Kingdom, Europe and other countries.

ISBN-13: 978–0–230–61711–7
ISBN-10: 0–230–61711–5

Library of Congress Cataloging-in-Publication Data
Officer, Lawrence H.
    Everyday economics : honest answers to tough questions / Lawrence
H. Officer.
        p. cm.
    ISBN 978–0–230–61711–7
    1. Economics.   I. Title.
HB171.O35   2009
330—dc22

                                                              2008051405

A catalogue record of the book is available from the British Library.

Design by Letra Libre, Inc.

First edition: May 2009
10 9 8 7 6 5 4 3 2 1
Printed in the United States of America.

DEDICATION

This book is dedicated to ordinary people,
who deserve to derive power from economics.

The ideas of economists and political philosophers, both when they are right and when they are wrong, are more powerful than is commonly understood. Indeed the world is ruled by little else.*

---

*John Maynard Keynes, *The General Theory of Employment, Interest and Money*. London: Macmillan, 1936, p. 383. Reproduced with permission of Palgrave Macmillan.

CONTENTS

ACKNOWLEDGMENTS

I have always believed that economics, if presented appropriately, can be used in practical ways to guide people's daily lives, in their thoughts and actions. That is how I teach principles of economics and intermediate economics to my students at University of Illinois at Chicago. I am grateful to those who encouraged me to write a book with that orientation. Laurie Harting, my editor at Palgrave Macmillan, bounced ideas back and forth with me until we jointly hit on the right tone and the right book, and she made excellent suggestions throughout the writing process. Donna Cherry, the Production Manager at Palgrave Macmillan, improved the book with input that went far beyond the usual expertise of a production specialist. My younger son, Ari Joseph Officer, graciously invited me to co-author an op-ed piece for TIME.com, which got me moving on the practical-economics writing track that resulted in *Everyday Economics*. My spouse, Sandra Diane Officer, provided good advice every step of the way and made many constructive comments that improved the book.

The expositions, descriptions, interpretations, opinions, conclusions, judgments, and other statements in this book are mine alone. The advice offered in this book comes with no guarantee other than sincerity. Readers who choose to adopt some or all of the advice, in original or modified form, do so at their own risk. The publisher and I disclaim any responsibility for the consequences.

Lawrence H. Officer
Glencoe, Illinois
December 2008

INTRODUCTION
(ECONOMICS
IS FOR YOU)

This chapter conveys the author's promise that *Everyday Economics* presents economics as something exciting for you to read about and something beneficial to you to apply. Your worst fears about the economy will be allayed, your grand illusions about the economy will be dispelled, and the usefulness of economics in your daily decision making will become obvious.

This book is for Everyman and Everywoman: Economics is for everyone. It is for people like you—educated, intelligent, and aware—who want to understand the world better and want to make the best decisions in their daily lives. That is why the book is called *Everyday Economics*. Many people think of economics as a dry, scholarly subject. But that is not the economics of this book. If life is exciting, then economics is exciting. If you want a better life, then economics is for you. You don't have to be an economist to understand how economics affects you. You don't have to be an economist to use economics to improve your life. *Everyday Economics* gives you an engaging way of looking at the world, and gives you practical advice on making financial decisions. If you believe the reputation of economics as being a boring subject to people who are not economists; if you think that economics deals only with events that are beyond your daily experiences, you are in for a pleasant surprise as you read this book.

Certainly a lot of reporting and talk in the media and blogs on the Internet have economics as a topic, often as the main topic. There is now so much "economic" information available that processing the information has become an important skill. One tends to forget that economics is primarily a technique, a way of thinking, rather than merely an accumulation of facts. Understanding economics, and especially knowing *how to apply economics,* would be to your advantage. The point of the book is to be useful to you, by helping you think though financial, consumer, national, and even global concerns. While this book may not drastically change your life, it can enhance your life. *Everyday Economics* will give you more control over your life, both in thought and deed, by changing your attitude and your behavior.

Knowledge is an intellectual and emotional power. There are economic forces all around you. Right now, you have either too much or too little concern about these forces. When should you worry about them? When should you relax? Sometimes you are worrying too much. This book will change your thinking about the economic environment so that you don't dwell on things unnecessarily. At other times you are not worried enough: You think that everything economic will turn out well.

Everyday Economics shows you how to put your current economic concerns into proper perspective: The book explains how to address the economic challenges that you face so the outcome is more to your advantage. You will gain greater confidence with the knowledge that you are legitimately concerned only about economic matters that warrant such attention, and that you are not wasting mental and emotional energy on economic fears that have no basis in reality.

There are two opposite kinds of illusions that people have. First, people think that the government usually makes the correct decisions in economic matters; that the government can be trusted to do the right thing economically; that the government at the very least has good intentions; and that, if the economic outcome is poor, then the government was up against economic forces beyond its control. Many parts of the book will show that assuming government is good in intentions, in actions, and in results is unrealistic. So swallow the right pill: It is time to break that illusion!

Sometimes the government adopts economic policies with the *intention* of helping only a small group in the economy. One example of this is the restrictions on the imports of sugar, set up purely to help the U.S. sugar industry, regardless of whether the rest of us suffer for it. Sometimes the government's intention is good, but the outcome is bad—for example, rent control in New York City. Both of these issues are considered and explained later in the book.

The second kind of illusion that people have is that there will be an "economic meltdown." Many people fear that the entire economy will go to pot and that their standard of living, if not civilization itself, will be driven down to an unacceptably low level. Could a depression of the magnitude of the Great Depression of the 1930s happen again? Could the stock market bust to zero? Will it be impossible for me (or my child) to find a job?

While each of these events is not logically impossible, they are all so unlikely that they are not worth worrying about. The Great Depression is not likely to recur, because governments and central banks have learned a lot about what went wrong during the Great Depression and also know much more about economics. Undoubtedly, they would act vigorously to prevent a depression from happening again. The stock market could not approach even close to zero, because stock prices are fundamentally based on the expected economic performance of the companies whose stocks are traded. And ultimately that performance comes from the country's resources—natural resources, physical capital (factories, office buildings, farms, machinery, equipment), technology, labor, and human capital (trained and educated labor) of the domestic economy—and from the productivity of these resources. For the American economy, these resources are strong, growing, and cemented by technological improvement. As far as job availability is concerned, a growing economy, combined with your own education, training, and motivation, is your ultimate guarantee. True, recessions mess things up, but only temporarily. All of these scary issues are treated in later chapters.

Economics is a guide for you to make the best decisions. That means the best decisions *for you*. Economics tells you how to use opportunities to your best advantage. An advantage means an achievement toward a goal. The economics way is the efficient way: You get the most advantage for a given cost, or you incur the least cost for a given advantage. For example, you want to buy the best possible flat-panel TV at a cost of $1,000, or you want to obtain a flat-panel TV with specific characteristics (for example, the screen size and resolution that you determine before you shop) for the lowest possible price.

You stipulate the goal. If you are a business, the goal could be to earn the highest profit that you can. If you are a consumer, the goal is probably to get the highest satisfaction from your purchases. For example, you want to pay the lowest possible price for a certain model car that you have decided to buy. Economics can certainly help you when making such major purchases as a new automobile. Buying (or selling) a car involves a lot of bargaining, and *Everyday Economics* shows you how to bargain effectively.

Economics is universal. The decision making based on economic thinking is applicable to any objective. The goal doesn't have to be self-centered. You could want to give as much money as possible to charity, or to publicize a charitable event as widely as possible with limited funds, and so on.

Everyday Economics does not approach economics as a dull, tedious subject. Rather, economics is an interesting and workable way of thinking and behaving—when presented in an interesting and workable way. That is accomplished by two features of this book. First, all chapters are presented as questions and answers, a format that focuses on the issues that concern you. Second, virtually all the questions are from real, everyday people just like you—people who are not economists, but who are intelligent and want to benefit from an economics that is oriented to their daily lives. These people were asked to be tough with their questions: no need to be polite; hit me with what you really want to know. Only a few questions were created by me, and these only for the sake of broader coverage of a chapter's topic.

Each question in the chapters is answered independent of every other question. This means that you don't need to read the book in order. You don't even have to read any chapter in order. If you want to concentrate on a particular topic, then turn to the appropriate chapter, but you can pick and choose among questions even within each chapter.

All the answers are mine alone. I don't sugar-coat anything—I tell the truth as I see it. I believe that the people reading this book want to know the truth, whether it is pleasant or unpleasant. They are brave and resourceful, and can face the economic truth. This book will help you deal with economic reality in your everyday life.

Everyday Economics will show you that economics is not only a fascinating topic but is also a useful tool that can help people in all walks of life make better decisions, from whether to buy an extended warranty on an electronic product to whether to support higher taxes on cigarettes. Economics cannot tell you everything about everything, and it cannot make you invincible. Economics is just a way of good thinking and a tool for advantageous decision making; that's all. But within those spheres—thought and decision making—economics can make you more powerful than you are now. *Everyday Economics* will help take you there. As you read this book you will find yourself better equipped both to handle the everyday matters that happen in your life and to understand the broad national and international issues that affect us all.

Chapter 1

MEANING OF ECONOMICS (REFINED COMMON SENSE)

Economics is approached as common sense. Many people see economics as just a lot of theories and interpretation of economic statistics. That kind of economics may be all right for academic economists, but it is not useful to you. *Everyday Economics* says you should begin with your common sense. Then, tweak your common sense so that it is oriented to an explicit goal for your own advantage and to the method of efficiency. You always want to reach your goal as efficiently as possible; that is, with the least expenditure of your resources.

What is economics?

A wise economist once stated that "economics is what economists do." You can't define economics easily, and certainly not in a way that is acceptable to all economists. Economists do many, many things. They are not concerned only with prices or only with business or only with government policy. Economics is not an accepted doctrine; it changes over time. What interested economists a century ago is not entirely the same as what interests them today.

Other observers have given economics a precise definition that goes something like this: *Economics is the study of scarcity; the concern of economics is anything that is scarce.* That means that the concern of economics could be money, energy, natural resources in general, time—anything at all, providing it is scarce. Scarcity, in terms of our definition, means that there is not enough of something to go around to satisfy all those who want it (whether individuals, businesses, governmental entities, and so on) and, in general, prices are determined to cut off the less-intense (excess) demand. Prices are set just high enough to remove the excess demand and purchases. Now, every entity (whether a person or an institution) gets just as much of the item as is wanted ("demanded"), because the entities that obtain that item are able and willing to pay for it. If it were available free of charge, there wouldn't be enough of it to go around. Of course, there are a few things that are not scarce: air, though it may be polluted, and water, though it may be contaminated. If you want (so-called pure) bottled water, you have to pay for it; so it, too, is scarce.

The definition of economics used above is often extended to incorporate decision making in the face of scarce resources. You can't do everything that you want; you can't get everything that you want. If you buy an automobile, then you can't go on a family vacation (since there is not enough money to do both). If you become a doctor, then you can't become an electrician (since there is not enough time to do both). Decisions on what to do and what to get mean that you are giving up things that you otherwise could do or could get. Economics studies such decision making, which is usually the decision making that we encounter. We live in a world of scarcity; rarely does a person, business, or government have a superabundance of items such that giving up certain things to get other things does not play an important role in decisions.

Some economists carry that definition further, so *economics is decision-making that not only involves allocating scarce resources to various use or uses but also is "rational."* Sometimes goals are inconsistent with one another. An individual can't save as much as possible *and* spend as much as possible. A business can't use the entirety of its profits to expand operations *and* to distribute as dividends. Sometimes goals are unachievable (for instance, no one can invent a perpetual motion machine). Inconsistent or unachievable goals are considered "irrational" by economists and so are outside the realm of economics.

So what is "rational behavior," according to economics? You are rational if you fulfill two requirements. First, you must have an objective that is internally consistent, or, for multiple goals, have objectives that are consistent with one another. Second, you must spend as few resources as possible to achieve your objective or objectives. In other words, you must take every opportunity to bring yourself closer to your goal, but in a resource-efficient way. That is an example of "economic efficiency."

Even if the ultimate objective happens to be unachievable, the objective could be to get *as close as possible* to the goal—and that is rational. Maybe your goal is to be the wealthiest person in the country. That objective is unattainable, but wanting to be as wealthy as possible is quite rational. The goal doesn't even have to be a selfish one. It could be to give as much of your money as you can to charity while maintaining your standard of living.

There is a serious criticism of the above definition, but it probably isn't what you think. You don't have to be selfish to be rational; so that's not the issue. The problem is that this definition—which has come to be the standard—encompasses all of *microeconomics* but not all of *macroeconomics*. Households and businesses, whether as individuals or as combined in a market, are the main subject of microeconomics—

and they make decisions under conditions of scarcity. In large part, the same applies to governments.

But sometimes the problem is not that there is too little of something, but that there is too much of it. Consider the following macroeconomic issue: When there is a recession, there are too few jobs for the number of available workers, thus resulting in unemployment. Note that the situation can be redefined to be a surplus of labor rather than a scarcity of jobs. But that is not logical in general, because it does not apply to scarcity in other contexts. For example, an "energy shortage" (better termed "energy scarcity") does not mean an abundance of something else.

Therefore other economists modify the definition to remove the "scarcity" context: *Economics is the study of rational decision making—period! Resources involved don't have to be scarce.* I happen to like this definition. Now both microeconomics and macroeconomics are covered. Also, economics is properly delineated. It isn't the study of anything in particular. Rather, it is the study of a particular kind of decision making, which seeks to attain a consistent objective as efficiently as possible. Just fulfill the objective in the best possible way, which generally means using the least amount of resources, but could mean something else. For example, increasing employment involves using up abundant labor. To meet the objective of increasing employment, there could be deliberate "make-work" programs that wouldn't succeed if "economic efficiency" were a requirement. The resulting increase in total economic output (GDP, or gross domestic product) might be "economically inefficient" in using up more workers than if there were not widespread unemployment—but it meets the objective.

⒬ What is the difference between microeconomics and macroeconomics?

Ⓐ The prefixes in micro- and macroeconomics have the same connotations as in common usage. "Micro" deals with small things; "macro" deals with big things. Concretely, microeconomics studies the decision making of individual consumers and individual businesses, whereas macroeconomics is concerned with the overall economy.

Examples of microeconomic questions are: How does the consumer decide to allocate his income between saving and spending budgets? How does he allocate his spending budget among goods and services (which goods and services to buy, and how much of each)? How does a person decide how many hours per week to work (assuming that he has the option of deciding on his hours)? At what age does an individual plan to retire?

On the business side, how does the firm decide which commodities to produce, and how many workers to hire, and with what skills? Under what circumstance would the firm engage in overtime work? How much machinery would the firm rent or purchase? When would the organization expand its physical plant or its size (number of factories or office space)—and by how much would it expand? What price would the firm charge for each commodity that it produces? How can managers be given proper incentives so that they make decisions in the best interests of the firm and the firm's owners (stockholders, if the firm is organized as a corporation)? The last question just might be the most important issue for a business, and it is addressed in later chapters.

Individual *markets*, that is, markets for individual commodities, are also within the realm of microeconomics: How are prices determined in a competitive market (one with many buyers and many sellers, each with a small market share, and with a homogeneous commodity)? In a monopolistic market (one seller of a product with no close substitute)? In an oligopoly (meaning just a few sellers) with an identical product (all firms producing the same commodity)? In an oligopoly with a differentiated product (each firm producing a somewhat different commodity, at least in the minds of consumers)?

Macroeconomics has to aggregate (combine magnitudes) to give meaningful answers to economy-wide questions. So, instead of the physical amount of a commodity, macroeconomics deals with the country's entire output (GDP) in real terms, meaning corrected over time for any inflation that takes place. Instead of considering the number of workers in one firm or one market, macroeconomics considers total employment in the economy, and total unemployment. Questions include: What makes GDP move in cycles ("the business cycle")? What determines how fast GDP grows ("economic growth")? What determines the amount of inflation? What causes changes in the exchange rate (price of the domestic country's currency in terms of the currency of another country, or, equivalently, the reverse)? All these macroeconomic questions are answered in later chapters.

Economists love to study government policy, whether under the rubric of microeconomics or macroeconomics. Microeconomic policy issues include: environmental protection; bailouts of individual firms; antitrust policy (meaning government action *against* the market power of monopolies and oligopolies); regulation of monopolies and oligopolies (meaning restrictions on their price and/or production); and price controls (under a micro setting, meaning for an individual industry). Macroeconomic policy issues include the workings of monetary and fiscal policy; the management of the government debt; and price controls (under a macro setting, controls encompassing a large part of the economy).

Some issues do not fit neatly into one category or the other. When the actions of one market affect the actions of another market, the issue could be either a microeconomic or a macroeconomic one. If, however, the markets are aggregated and therefore large (for example, agriculture and manufacturing), then the issue is clearly within the realm of macroeconomics.

Contrary to what you may think, microeconomics has a much more solid foundation than macroeconomics does. This is so despite the fact that macroeconomic issues tend to be the "big" and important issues in economics. And economists are in stronger agreement regarding microeconomic issues than macroeconomic issues. Disclosure: I teach both microeconomics and macroeconomics, and I myself prefer microeconomics, because I believe that microeconomics provides a more useful way of understanding reality.

Microeconomics is a solid body of knowledge, because it is based on behavior of individual people. Households and businesses are run by people, and people are directly affected by the decisions that they make for the households and businesses that they operate. Therefore understanding how people behave is the logical way of understanding how households and businesses behave.

In contrast, macroeconomics deals with large entities in which decision makers are not directly affected by what they do. Macroeconomics is not directly based on the rational behavior of individuals paying the consequences of their own actions. So macroeconomics lacks the solid foundation of microeconomics. It should not be surprising that the macroeconomics specialists are still working things out, whether in explaining how the economy works (recessions, economic expansions, inflation, unemployment) or in assessing governmental (monetary and fiscal) policies.

ⓠ How can economics, being a science, be exciting for me to learn about?

Ⓐ Economics is not in the realm of physical or biological science. Rather, it is a *social* science. *Economics studies the behavior of human beings within society—and that is what makes economics fascinating.* Human beings are much more interesting to study than atoms or chemical elements. One reason is that we are studying ourselves, so we are really involved. A second reason is that, as we know from personal experience, human behavior is not as predictable as the physical world. Total predictability can be totally boring.

A third reason why economics is fascinating is that human beings can, and have, changed the environment in which they live. In fact, they have radically changed that environment. A fourth reason is that economics itself, by studying the behavior of human beings within society, can alter that behavior. In turn, the altered behavior affects economics as a discipline. If all that sounds circular and therefore weird, you are in good company—economists find that this situation requires particular attention to be dealt with satisfactorily.

Q Don't successful businesspeople operate on intuition? So is economics really useful for businesspeople?

A Successful businesspeople do use their intuition, their intelligence, and their experience to make decisions. But economics could add something to the repertoire of businesspeople that goes beyond these eminently desirable qualities. Here is a story that I always tell when I appear before a group of businesspeople.

> Two people are in a balloon flying low over a rural area; two other people are on the ground below. The folks in the balloon lean over and together yell out, "Where are we?" The people below respond in unison, "You're in a balloon."
>
> Then two conversations take place simultaneously. One person in the balloon says to the other, "See these people below, I know their profession." The other person asks, "What is their profession?" The first person answers, *"They're economists."* Second person: "Why do you say that?" First person: *"Because they just state the obvious."*
>
> Meanwhile, on the ground below, one person says to the other, "See those people in the balloon, I know their profession." The other person asks, "What is their profession?" The first person answers, *"They're businesspeople."* Second person: "Why do you say that?" First person: *"Because they see everything, but they don't know where they are."*

The story illustrates several different points regarding economists and businesspeople. First, economics should be useful; it should give people a different perspective on things. If economics only confirms and supports the way people ordinarily think and act, then it would have no benefit except to scholars, and I would not have written this book. Second, businesspeople can be so involved with their day-to-day operations that they don't take a broader view and try to understand what is going on. Economics can certainly be of use in that process. And third, economists and businesspeople have a lot to learn from each other. Economists in the academic world in particular should not study and teach in a cocoon. They should get out in the real world and see what is going on. That is the best way to make economics more relevant to all of us.

Q What can learning about economics do for me?

A A common line that economics professors use on their students is: "Economics may not keep you out of the unemployment line, but at least you'll know why you're there."

The idea is that, while economics is not practical, it does help make you an informed person. I agree that economics helps you understand the world; but economics can give you much more than that. I firmly believe that economics lives! Economics not only helps you understand the world around you; it also orients your thought processes so that you make decisions that are to your advantage. Economics is a practical body of knowledge—for both thought and action. That philosophy underlies *Everyday Economics.*

You don't have to study economics formally in order to apply it to your daily life. Economics is a way of understanding the world and a way of making sound decisions. What is that way? Basically, economics is a kind of common sense; more than just intuition and a bit deeper and a bit broader than your ordinary common sense. As a great economist once put it, "economics is *refined* common sense." Let's be practical and discuss using economics to make better decisions in your life.

First of all, you should be goal-oriented. If you want to make a good decision, you have to know exactly what your objective is. What are you trying to accomplish? That is one ingredient in a good (what economists call a "rational") decision. Second, you should be concerned with the limited resources—for example, the limited money or limited time—at your disposal. So, you'll want to watch these resources carefully, and use as few resources as possible to reach your objective, because you will need your time and your money for a lot of other things. That is the second ingredient in a rational decision.

It is possible to follow these rules subconsciously, but you are much more likely to incorporate them and apply them correctly in your decision making if you do so consciously and explicitly. The little bit of extra effort required for conscious rational decision making could give you a tremendous advantage in your life.

ⓠ What are the "tools" of economics? Any implication for my investment decisions?

🅐 Economics makes use of a variety of tools, many taken from other disciplines. Mathematics facilitates the expression of economic theories and the deduction of implications of these theories. Mathematics does not have to be algebraic; mere graphs are helpful in many situations. History provides a vast amount of experience to help in both developing and testing economic theories. Econometrics (statistical procedures oriented to economics) is invaluable for the testing of economic theories. Experimental economics, involving laboratory or computer experiments, is another approach to developing and testing theories. Finally, just thinking about how to explain economic phenomena is also a tool of economics.

Everyone knows about mathematics, graphs, and history. Here is an example of econometrics used in investment decisions. Suppose you are interested in purchasing the stock of a gold-producing company. Your investment advisor, if a quantitative type, could gather statistics on the price of gold and the stock price of the gold-producing company. He might discover that when the price of gold goes up by 10 percent, the stock price goes up by 40 percent. Now all that the investment advisor has to do is forecast the future price of gold so that you buy *in advance* of the price rise of gold and the price rise of the stock. That forecast is not easy to do, but it is a lot easier than directly predicting the price of a particular stock.

As for experimental economics, whether the subjects are human beings or animals, let us leave aside ethical issues, which reasonable people certainly could have. The fact is that these experiments are just that—experiments. An experiment is not the same thing as reality. The best laboratory that economists have is the real world. That is where real things happen to real people, for real reasons.

The economic theories that result from the application of some or all of the various tools of economics are often presented in a very complex way, especially if mathematics is involved. I believe that a foolish result can be hidden by complexity. My own position is that if a theory cannot be exposited in simple and clear language, and if, in that form, it is not persuasive as an explanation of the economic phenomenon under consideration, then the theory should either be rejected outright or put on hold.

Regarding the second question, I offer the same advice regarding complex investment assets. You ought to be suspicious of outlets for your investment that are so complex or presented in so complicated a manner that they are beyond your understanding. If you have to trust someone else for the understanding, especially if that person is brokering the investment outlet, then do not be fooled by the investment being touted. Believe me, many a wealthy individual and many a pension fund and many a municipality have suffered financially from unwise investments in which the broker or other advisor promised high expected return but neglected to emphasize the associated high risk of loss.

Q What are the principal "schools of thought" in economics?

A The two main streams of thought in economics revolve around the extent to which the private economy is well functioning and what the consequent role of government should be. The two schools of thought, in their mainstream forms, are Keynesianism and the Chicago School.

Keynesianism is named after John Maynard Keynes, a British economist who in 1936 wrote an important economics book, *The General Theory of Employment, Interest and Money,* and is quoted in the dedication of *Everyday Economics.* He had many followers who interpreted his work and continued the development of his economic analysis and policy views. Keynesianism is based on the view that the economy, if left alone, will sometimes have recessions (perhaps even depressions, meaning serious recessions) with high levels of unemployment and will sometimes have over-employment (a "heated economy" straining beyond capacity) and consequent inflation. The government should fight recessions by increasing government spending on goods and services and by reducing taxes on individuals and businesses—what is called expansionary fiscal policy. A recession should lead to an active government budget deficit. The goal of balancing the budget, even as a long-run average over time, is viewed as an impediment to sound fiscal policy and is therefore rejected.

Monetary policy is considered a useful accompaniment to fiscal policy. In a recession or depression, expansion of the money supply is advocated. The central bank increases the growth rate of the money supply in order to reduce interest rates and thereby stimulate business investment of physical items (construction, machinery, equipment) and household purchases of newly constructed homes. But monetary policy is viewed as having limited effectiveness, for three reasons. First, there is a limit to how far the interest rate can be pushed down (it can't go below zero). Second, even though their lending capacity is expanded, banks cannot be *forced* to make loans to businesses and households (enabling their investment and home purchases). Third, there may be a general lack of confidence in the economy, such that not only banks but also businesses and households are pessimistic about the future of the economy, and thus the businesses and households may not want to invest or buy homes—even if banks are willing to lend.

Logically, in an inflationary period, fiscal and monetary policy should be contractionary—simply a reversal of the expansionary policies. However, inflation in the modern economy can go along with recession; this is called "stagflation." With stagflation, monetary policy and fiscal policy are pulled in opposite directions. Some Keynesians recommend "incomes policy" in this situation: the government would limit increases in wages and prices by direct policy. Most economists view that as an extreme measure. Other Keynesian policies generally considered extreme are a "mixed economy" (ownership of industry by government as much as by private parties) and a "welfare state" (the government ensuring that all residents receive a basic package of goods and services—food, clothing, shelter, education, and health care).

Some critics of Keynesianism view the welfare state as being on the road to socialism.

The *Chicago School* is associated with the economics faculty at the University of Chicago and evolved over a period that began in the 1930s. The Chicago School view of monetary and fiscal policy is quite different from the Keynesian view. Conventional fiscal policy is considered largely ineffective by the Chicago School. Reason: As the government borrows to finance the budget deficit, interest rates are pushed up, and private spending (business investment and household purchases of homes) is discouraged; government spending "crowds out" private spending. While monetary policy is effective, the timing of its impact on the economy is highly unpredictable. Thus, followers of the Chicago School are also "monetarists" who suggest that the government and central bank give up trying to fine-tune the economy. Instead, fiscal policy should be conducted from the standpoint of long-run economic efficiency, and monetary policy should follow a simple rule of increasing the money supply at a constant rate of growth irrespective of the state of the economy.

In general, members of the Chicago School see the private, free-market economy as well functioning on its own and want minimal government intervention. They are strong advocates of free trade both domestically and internationally. Some economists take the Chicago School to an extreme and adopt "libertarianism," under which the role of government in regulating private behavior is almost nonexistent. Libertarians could support children "divorcing" their parents, virtually zero taxes, no public education, and so on. In fairness to the Chicago School, a case could be made that libertarianism emanates rather from the philosophy ("objectivism") found in the writings of Ayn Rand (author of *The Fountainhead, Atlas Shrugged,* and other works), but she herself did not accept that honor! Some critics of the Chicago School see extreme libertarianism as its logical progression.

An economy such as the United States is a "mixed economy," exhibiting traits of both Keynesianism and the Chicago School. Which school of thought is dominant depends heavily on which political party is in power in Washington. The Democratic Party is associated with Keynesianism and the Republican Party with the Chicago School.

Q Aren't economists concerned about just the way things are and not about the way things ought to be?

A There are people who criticize what economists do by saying that "an economist knows the price of everything and the value of nothing." That statement is a takeoff on a quotation from nineteenth-century playwright and author Oscar Wilde, who wrote: "What is a cynic? A man who knows the price of everything and the value of nothing."

One way to interpret the criticism is that economists are cynics. But that is a false generalization. There is variation among economists just as there is among any group of people. Some economists are cynics, some are idealists.

Economists usually interpret the criticism in another way. They consider the criticism to be that economists are amoral; that an economist is concerned only with the way things are and not with the way things ought to be. It is not that economists are bad people; they simply *don't care* whether the economy (or any part of the economy) is good or bad.

From the standpoint of economics as a science, there is truth in the statement. Economics as a science looks at reality and tries to explain things without making moral judgments. However, economists are more than scientists. Economists certainly make a lot of moral judgments about the economy and especially offer a lot of policy recommendations. Economists do not restrict themselves to economics as a science. So the criticism is inaccurate.

Q Why can't economists agree among themselves as to what to do about the economy?

A A saying sometimes directed at economists goes like this: "If you laid all the economists of the world end-to-end, they would not reach a conclusion." This quotation criticizes economists for having so many different views and making so many different policy recommendations about the same issue.

The quotation is largely unfair. There are so many things that economists are in virtually complete agreement about. Examples: Rent control is economically inefficient; technological improvement is important for economic growth; tariffs usually protect inefficient industries; sales taxes are detrimental to the poor, compared to income taxes; and on and on.

It is true that economists do disagree sometimes. When economists disagree, it is either because they do not quite see the world in the same way and are uncertain which theory fits, or because they have different value judgments (statements of desirability). For example, some want to tax the rich more, to redistribute income to the poor; others want to tax the rich less, to induce them to work harder and invest more, thus stimulating economic growth. The first prescription has the underlying value judgment that helping the poor is more important than economic growth; the second prescription has the reverse value judgment. A problem that many economists have is that they do not make their value judgments explicit—so it is often unclear which of their statements are objectively oriented ("scientific") and which are based on a value judgment.

Chapter 2

EMPLOYMENT AND COMPENSATION (LABOR MARKETS AND YOU)

Jobs, careers, pay, unemployment—if economics has anything at all to offer, it should do so in the area of work, which affects so many of us for a good third of the Monday-to-Friday component of the week. *Everyday Economics* doesn't just help us understand the issues regarding work and pay; it also guides us in our career decision-making, and that of our children.

Q With overseas outsourcing and increased foreign competition for jobs, how do I help guide my children into jobs and careers that will thrive in the United States?

A Your children will have to be more flexible than you. It may not be possible for your children to have great job satisfaction, *and* earn a high income, *and* live near you. With the globalization of the economy, it is even possible that your children will have to live outside the country, at least for part of their careers, if a particular job and a high salary are of supreme importance to them. In general, outsourcing and loss of jobs to overseas mean that your children will be faced with less stability in their jobs and even in their careers. In response to this work environment, flexibility is the key. Your children would be wise to be prepared to relocate and, if necessary, reeducate or retrain—for the sake of their economic success.

Certainly, you want your children to have a certain level of happiness, both in their work and in their personal lives. No doubt, they also want their happiness. This means that, as a minimum, your children should choose careers in which they are not unhappy. Most people spend one-third of the weekdays in their work environment. To be unhappy in your job can make your whole life miserable. But the objective cannot reasonably be the greatest possible happiness. Your children will probably want to have an occupation with earning power, another important objective.

It would be nice if job satisfaction and earning power could always go together. Sometimes they do. As the saying goes, "happy is the person whose vocation is also her avocation." Unfortunately, there is sometimes a trade-off between a career that provides job satisfaction and a career with high earning power. Often, in economic decisions, we have to compromise among several objectives. In this case, the objectives are job satisfaction, income, and location. The trick here is to have a minimum of each objective: a certain amount of job satisfaction, a certain level of income, and an acceptable location. Then, having satisfied the minimum for each goal, you can try to achieve more than the minimum for one or more of these goals.

From an economic standpoint, paramount to achieving all three career objectives are education, training, and job experience. These are what economists call "investment in human capital." Your child is adding marketable skills to her innate capacity for work. For a young child, the best way to do this is by fostering her interests and encouraging her motivation for learning. Of course, formal education plays an important role. Many parents believe that acceptance into the very best school system is a sound strategy for continued educational, and ultimately occupational, success. In fact, more important than where a child attends high school are her study habits and thirst for knowledge.

When your child goes to college, what should be the focus of study? It is useful for your child to know the difference between "general human capital" and "specific human capital"—even if she doesn't know that economic lingo. "General human capital" means education or training that is applicable to a large number of occupations; "specific human capital" is applicable to just one or to a very limited number of occupations. Examples of subjects that provide "general human capital" are philosophy, literature, and law. Examples of subjects that provide specific human capital include medicine (or pre-med), nursing, and engineering. The fundamental choice for a college major is between a field that provides general human capital versus one that offers specific human capital.

As a general rule (though it is not always true), the advantage of a college major involving general human capital is flexibility of occupations, while the advantage of a major providing specific human capital is greater earning power in that one occupation (or group of occupations).

Your children don't have to go to a university to acquire human capital. *Training* is a good way to obtain specific capital. Carpentry, plumbing, mechanics, and electrical work are examples of specific human-capital skills acquired in trade school. These occupations can be both high-paying and job-satisfying. In my previous location, my plumber had graduated with an M.A. in English and began teaching. He later left the teaching profession to train as a plumber and was so successful in his new occupation that he formed his own company.

My plumber's success is an example to be emulated by those with proper abilities. "Entrepreneurship" involves forming new firms, creating new products or new technology and putting them to practical use, developing new uses for existing products, finding new markets, and so on. Some people drop out of college to give full rein to their entrepreneurship—think Microsoft's Bill Gates. Imagine how Gates's parents reacted when he told them he was leaving Harvard without a degree! If your child is entrepreneurial, do not be upset if formal schooling is not the path that she chooses. She may be very successful jumping into the business world without a complete traditional education.

However, most of us lack entrepreneurial skills (which, in my opinion, are innate and therefore cannot be acquired). From an income-earning standpoint, we want our children to choose careers for which there will be many high-paying and satisfying jobs. What to choose? No one can predict the future for specific occupations, but here are a few ideas.

People are living longer, so there will be more elderly people as time goes on. Therefore, there will be more need for goods and services that cater to an older population. These commodities include medical care, retirement communities, classes and special activities for seniors, home delivery of commodities, and so on. The implication is that the geriatric health field will be growing for the foreseeable future, and, therefore, preparing for a career in that field makes good economic sense. Because the United States will have an increased elderly population, geriatric health-care skills are very likely to be in high demand and thus offer a high-paying and possibly very satisfying career option.

Conversely, if the population becomes younger (since the birth rate is going up and the immigration of young families is increasing), then there will be higher production of products that appeal to a younger generation and will create more job opportunities in that area.

These products include electronic devices, fashionable clothing, recreational services, and so on. It is also possible to have a population explosion at both the lower and upper ends of the age range. In this case, choosing a career in a youth-oriented field could also be high-paying and satisfying.

It is very likely that environmental concerns will become more and more important. There will be greater production of environmentally friendly ("green") commodities: electric cars, solar heating devices, anti-pollution equipment, noiseless or low-noise lawnmowers, nontoxic cleaning products, wind energy, organic food, energy-efficient office spaces, and so on. There will be great opportunities not only for related occupations but also for entrepreneurship. It is possible that entrepreneurship oriented to green technology will give rise to the next group of billionaires. The countries that first push for "green" industries will be sources of scientific, engineering, legal, accounting, and related professional jobs. If the United States is not among these countries, your environmentally oriented child might have to work elsewhere for job satisfaction and high income.

Some final advice: For young people especially, an important way to develop some basic "general human capital" is job experience. For high-school students, summer and part-time jobs and internships (providing the time commitment does not interfere with school and study time) are great ways to obtain "general human capital" in the form of good work habits: promptness, cooperation, respect for coworkers and customers, and motivation to do one's very best both in the workplace and in daily life.

Why are earnings so disproportionate to contribution to society? For example, teachers and social workers earn so much less than professional athletes and movie stars.

We have to separate (1) the reasons why wages are different from (2) the issue of whether it is fair for them to be different. The difference in wages is due to demand and supply. Professional athletes and movie stars have special abilities that are rare among the population and are in market demand. These genetically lucky people have precise eye-to-hand coordination or can run fast or have huge muscle mass, or they are beautiful or ruggedly handsome or can feign behavior so that their acting appears realistic. The point is that the great majority of people lack these rare abilities. No matter how much we practice or study, we can't succeed as professional athletes or movie stars. So the supply of people with the ability to be professional athletes and movie stars is fairly low. It is hard to replace these workers with people of equal abilities, because only a limited number of these people are available. It is not surprising that top athletes and movie stars insist on high wages and get away with it.

In contrast, almost anyone willing to "invest" time and money in the required education can become a teacher or a social worker. This investment in teaching and social work skills is commendable from the standpoint of society, but it means that the supply of teachers and social workers can be quite high. It follows that a teacher or social worker who insists on a higher than market wage can easily be replaced. When more teachers or social workers are wanted, there is a fairly large pool from which to choose.

Having a rare ability is of no economic use unless there is a demand for it. And the demand for professional athletes and actors and actresses—at least the demand for the *top* people in these professions—is very high. Why? The reason is that those who hire these people can make a lot of money by putting them to work. They make this money because a large number of average people—like you and me—are willing to pay money to watch professional athletic events (in person or on television) and films with movie stars, to pay for cable TV to see these events, and to tolerate a lot of commercials to watch these things on television.

The point is that the top athletes and movie stars generate a lot of money for professional team owners and movie studios. The situation of teachers and social workers is different. The demand for their services is not as high because they do not bring in anywhere near that amount of money to those who employ them. In addition, the employers of teachers and social workers are generally the public sector—school systems and governments—and the public sector traditionally pays lower wages than the private sector. But that is a minor point.

The bottom line is that there is a high demand and low supply for top athletes and actors and actresses, but a low demand and high supply for teachers and social workers. Economics tells us that the resulting wage for the first group will be much higher than for the second group.

It is economic efficiency when occupations in high demand and low supply get a high wage while occupations in low demand and high supply get a low wage. If the government decided to equalize the wages of both groups, or even to move them somewhat closer together, the economy would have too few athletes and actors and actresses and too many teachers and social workers. (I mean "too few" and "too many" from the standpoint of economic efficiency.)

What about the fairness issue? There does appear to be something wrong with a situation in which athletes and actors and actresses, who after all perform only recreational services, earn so much more money than teachers and social workers, who are vital in educating our young people and in helping people with serious problems. But that is the market system at work. If you like, you can blame the market system for the unfairness.

Following the dictates of demand and supply generally results in economic efficiency, as it does in this case. But the outcome is not necessarily "fair." Society could decide that fairness is more important than efficiency. For instance, the government could set a "wage floor" (the lowest allowable wage) for teachers and social workers, and also set a "wage ceiling" (the highest allowable wage) for athletes and actors and actresses. Or, the government could tax the earnings of athletes and actors and actresses and give the proceeds to teachers and social workers.

Either option would make wages "fairer" all around, but would lead to too many people wanting to be teachers and social workers instead of preparing for other jobs of greater importance to the economy (from the standpoint of efficiency). It is also possible that the fairly unique abilities of professional athletes and actors and actresses are not transferable to other occupations, and that, even if their earnings were reduced, they would put in as many hours and work just as hard in their occupations as they do now. Then there would be just as much supply of people in these occupations as without the wage ceiling. If that were the case, then the reduction in economic efficiency would not happen at the upper end of the wage scale (for professional athletes and movie stars), but it would still be important at the lower end (for teachers and social workers).

Q Is there still discrimination against females and minorities in terms of getting a job, obtaining a promotion, and achieving a salary level the same as that of white males for a particular position? How do we make sure that equally productive workers are treated equally in the job market, irrespective of the gender or racial group to which a worker belongs?

A The very visible women and minorities in the highest positions in government, businesses, and universities would seem to suggest that there is no more discrimination in the United States. Unfortunately, discrimination still exists and active policy on the part of both government and private business will be required to eradicate it.

To answer your question adequately, we should first understand the meaning of discrimination in the labor market. Discrimination is an overt action or inaction. You are a victim of discrimination if, *because of the group to which you belong:* (1) your wage is below the wage of an equally productive worker in the same job; (2) you are not hired for a particular job, even though you are at least as qualified as the person who did get the job; or (3) you do not get a promotion for which you have equal or better qualifications than the person who did. Discrimination can be against groups identified by race, religion, age, height, weight, gender, gender preference, immigration status, and so on. There are two possible causes of discrimination: prejudice and statistics.

Discrimination can be due to prejudice. *Prejudice means that you do not like someone because of the group to which he or she belongs.* This prejudice can be on the part of workers (called "worker discrimination"; for example, male workers may refuse to work with female coworkers or have female managers) or on the part of firms through their managers (called "firm discrimination"; for example, firms may refuse to hire members of racial minorities for certain positions).

Discrimination can also occur even when prejudice is not involved. This is called "statistical discrimination." It happens when the firm (acting through its managers) assigns the worker or prospective worker a productivity level equal to *the average productivity of the group to which the worker belongs.* For example, a high-school dropout might be expected to have the average absentee history of all high-school dropouts and therefore would not be hired, even though she *as an individual* in fact would be conscientious about showing up for work.

Interestingly, there can also be prejudice without discrimination. For instance, your manager doesn't like you because of the group to which you belong, but nevertheless hires or promotes you because you are so productive that she knows that you would substantially reduce the firm's costs or increase the firm's revenue.

My favorite example of this phenomenon is Jack Johnson, the first black boxing heavyweight champion. (You have to go back over a hundred years to when he became champion.) There was tremendous prejudice against Jack Johnson, and he was profoundly disliked, not only because he dared to take away what was then viewed by many as the epitome of white male supremacy (the boxing heavyweight championship) but also because of his flamboyant lifestyle and his habit of smiling every time he knocked out an opposing boxer. Yet the prejudice, horrible as it was, was not used to keep Jack Johnson from the ring. Johnson was not a victim of discrimination, at least for part of his boxing career. He was allowed to ply his trade and earned (and spent) a fortune, as have many boxers, irrespective of race.

Economics tells us that there is a "market solution" to *discrimination based on prejudice*. Such discriminating firms do so at a cost: inefficient production, higher costs of production, and lower profit. Firms that do not hire more productive individuals who are women or minorities in favor of less productive individuals who are male or white will have higher costs than non-discriminating firms and, *in a competitive environment*, will eventually go bankrupt unless they stop discriminating. The market works!

Unfortunately, this argument does not apply to firms with market power, or those that do not have effective competition. A monopoly firm is an extreme example of a firm that is able to discriminate without going bankrupt. However, these firms do pay a price for the discrimination: Their costs are higher and their profits lower than if they did not discriminate. Where firms are run by owners, the detrimental consequences of discrimination to the owners' profits are obvious, and discrimination often would not even arise.

If corporate managers (who are not the owners) are engaging in discrimination, then the stockholders (acting through the board of directors) logically should object to the resultant lower profits, and there is good hope that the discrimination will thereupon cease. Stockholders own the firm (the corporation), and managers who discriminate are reducing the corporation's profits, dividends, and stock-price increase. So there is good reason to believe that discrimination based on prejudice would be largely eliminated due to market forces alone.

Statistical discrimination is another matter. It can be rational for the firm to discriminate under that circumstance. It is sometimes costly or even impossible to form an accurate judgment of a prospective worker's productivity. Statistical discrimination is a cost-effective way of making a quick judgment of productivity. Managers may believe, with reason, that elderly people are more prone to use sick days, which would be to the detriment of the firm. A specific elderly person might be in superb health; nevertheless, the firm has no way of knowing that. Therefore, the average health pattern of the group (all elderly people) is assigned to that one elderly individual. *Note that prejudice is not involved in this discrimination.*

Another example concerns women of child-bearing age. These workers could decide to have children and take time off from work accordingly, again to the detriment of the firm. It is possible that the person in question will take minimum time off from work during and after her pregnancy; it is also possible that she will not choose to become pregnant while she is at the firm—but the firm doesn't know any of these things. So, if there are two workers equally qualified and one is a woman of child-bearing age, it is rational (but unfair) for the firm to give the job to the other person.

There are two policies that work to thwart discrimination effectively. Antitrust policy—breaking up monopolies and curbing the market power of firms in order to foster competition—acts to end discrimination based on prejudice (even though that result is only incidental). Family-leave policies, such as parental (both maternal and paternal) leave, work against the most prevalent type of statistical discrimination, which is that directed against women of child-bearing age. Unfortunately, family-leave policies are not universally so enlightened.

Fortunately, there exists a policy that has far greater impact on discrimination than antitrust policy and family leave. That policy is "investment in human capital." Human capital means the education and training embodied in human labor. The very visible success of *well-educated* females and minorities is proof of that assertion. Experts urge—and I believe them—that education must start at a very young age to take hold, and this means kindergarten and even pre-school. The problems to overcome are poverty and family structure, much more than race or gender.

The good news is that women are closing the "wage gap" with men, at least in the 20–30 age group. This is because women, on average, are becoming more and more educated compared to men. More women than men are attending college, and the change in social mores has made it acceptable for females to work at virtually every occupation in the economy. At one time, the great majority of working women opted for only a few occupations—nursing, teaching, and secretarial work—because these were considered to be the only "normal" (socially acceptable) occupations for women. (Of course, some women overrode social convention and became physicians, lawyers, even policewomen—but they were not many.)

Another change in social mores has made it acceptable for *married* middle-class women to work at all. At one time, it was not considered "normal" or "respectable" for middle-class women to continue to work after marriage.

To say that things have changed is the understatement of the century! Now women are present in virtually every occupation in the economy, and a high percentage of married women participate in the workforce. There are two economic reasons why married women can readily work outside the home. The widespread use of time-saving equipment for housework (refrigerators, washing and drying machines, and so on) makes housework both easier and less time-consuming. The existence of supermarkets, and superstores in general, where a person can purchase all groceries (and many other items) at one location, has had the same effect. These economic factors have merged with a changing social culture that expects married men to do more and more of their share of work in operating the household. *But the fact that women became more educated is the fundamental reason why they have entered into just about every occupation in the economy.*

Returning to discrimination against minorities, it is a sad fact that, if a white and a minority job applicant are both high-school dropouts or both just high-school graduates, the white person is much more likely to be hired. That is discrimination—whether statistic- or prejudice-based. As both applicants have more and more "human capital" in the form of education and training, the discrimination lessens, and then vanishes. That is why minorities who are professionally qualified have made it in the economy.

Antidiscrimination laws and affirmative-action programs are uncertain in their effectiveness and in any event have largely run their course. Workers, parents, and governments should concentrate on education and training. Embodying human capital in workers and future workers is the surest way to end discrimination and, at the same time, improve economic efficiency and enhance economic growth.

Q **Does economics have anything to say about executive compensation? In particular, will paying CEOs less money and offering fewer benefits cause American companies to become uncompetitive?**

A Yes to the first part of the question: Economics does have something to say about that. Economists believe that, in general, a chief executive officer (CEO) of a corporation should be paid in an incentive manner so that her decisions are in the best interests of the corporation. Ideally, the CEO's objective should be to maximize the long-run profits of the firm. If the CEO is paid only a fixed salary, she has no incentive (beyond ethics) to be entrepreneurial in behavior, meaning to innovate in products, production, and markets—which means to be inventive in a practical way for the good of the firm. Rather, she may simply play it safe, act as a day-to-day manager, just do the same old thing, and contentedly collect her salary.

To achieve entrepreneurial behavior, CEO compensation should have, and generally does have, built-in "incentive clauses." Examples are bonuses based on performance (for example, bonuses linked to the firm's profits or stock price). In the same vein, stock options are also part of the incentive package, and they can be extremely profitable if the firm's stock price shoots up. The problem here is that CEOs may concentrate too much on the short run—profits this year or the next year, stock price right now or in the near future—to the detriment of the firms' long-run profits and long-run stock price. In fairness to CEOs, stockholders in firms (as well as investors in general and investment advisors) do tend to be overly concerned with current profits or earnings and immediate stock prices. If CEOs are under pressure from these sources they would have to be unusually determined and courageous to adopt a long-run perspective.

CEOs are appointed, and their compensation packages arranged, by a corporation's board of directors, which is elected by the stockholders. In many corporations, the CEO is also chairman of the board. This gives her additional power within the corporation. Conventional wisdom, which is probably correct, is that the board of directors sometimes fails to supervise the CEO sufficiently, to the detriment of the stockholders, whom the board serves.

Turning to the second part of the question, both economics and common sense suggest that "you get what you pay for." A top-notch executive would command higher compensation than executives with less experience, less knowledge, and less proven results. If a corporation tries to save immediate money by paying less and obtaining a less-productive CEO, the company's profits, stock price, and perhaps even its very continued existence as an independent entity could be threatened. The company would become less competitive. If this practice were to occur on a large scale, American business as a whole could lose competitiveness.

However, there are situations in which the CEO is overpaid by legal or economic standards. The board could be bamboozled by a persuasive CEO candidate who turns out to have little substance. A CEO could illegally strip the firm of assets, or engage in personal behavior that damages the firm's reputation. The board should do its research before hiring a CEO, should be careful that the employment contract contains only proper incentives, and should supervise the CEO's behavior.

◻ The government tells us that the unemployment rate is only 6 percent of the workforce. But it seems that a good number of my friends are without jobs. Does the official figure underestimate actual unemployment? And where does the official figure come from?

◻ Let's take the last part of the question first. The U.S. official unemployment figure is computed and released monthly by the Bureau of Labor Statistics (BLS), which is part of the Department of Labor. Ideally, every person in the country of working age would be canvassed to see if he or she is unemployed; but that would be expensive and impractical. In fact, it is not even necessary. The BLS samples about sixty thousand households every month. With representation from every part of the country and sophisticated statistical techniques, the unemployment figure that results is very close to what a full census would measure *using the BLS definition of unemployment.* The questions that households are asked pertain to their situation during the month's "reference week," which means the week that includes the twelfth of the month.

The best way to understand the BLS definition is to realize that every person is placed into one (and only one) of four categories, depending on his or her situation during the reference week:

1. *Not in the civilian noninstitutional population 16 years old and over:* This category consists of people younger than 16, people on active duty in the military, and people who are institutionalized (such as in prisons or mental hospitals). If you are in one of these groups, then the BLS has no interest in you, at least for computation of unemployment.

2. *Employed:* This category includes people with jobs during the reference week. Included are people who worked for pay, even for only one hour, and "unpaid family workers" (relatives working for free in a family business or in a family firm) who worked at least 15 hours. Also included are people who have jobs but are not working during the reference week for various reasons, including vacation, illness, labor-management disputers, bad weather, and the like.

3. *Unemployed:* This category includes people without jobs *and* who actively looked for work in the four weeks prior to the reference week *and* who are currently available for work. Also in this category are workers who have been temporarily laid off from their jobs, even if they are not looking for alternative employment. If you have not actively looked for a job in the prior four weeks, you will not be counted in this category. Reading the want ads in newspapers or Googling job opportunities on the Internet is insufficient evidence of an active job search, which must include actions such as completing applications,

sending out resumes, having interviews, contacting friends or employment centers, and so on.

4. *Not in labor force:* This category consists of those who are without jobs and are not looking for jobs. It includes people who go to school full-time, people who are retired or have family responsibilities, people who have disabilities that prevent them from employment, and people who have simply given up looking for work.

The "labor force" is the sum of the number employed (category 2) and the number unemployed (category 3). Unemployment (technically, the "unemployment rate") is the percent of the labor force that is unemployed—category 3 as a percent of the sum of categories 2 and 3. Note that those outside the civilian noninstitutional population (category 1) and those not in the labor force (category 4) are ignored in the calculation of the unemployment rate.

Now to consider your main question, which is whether the official unemployment rate underestimates actual unemployment. Most economists would agree that it does. The main reason economists think that the BLS unemployment figure is too low is that "discouraged workers," those who want to work but out of frustration have given up looking for a job, are placed in category 4, rather than in the labor force. That doesn't make much sense. Another reason is that part-time workers are counted as employed and in the same category as full-time workers. It's as if the part-time workers were fully employed, ignoring the fact that some part-time workers would prefer full-time work but are unable to procure it and so must settle for part-time work instead. In my view, that also makes no sense. Yet a third reason is that some people may be only temporarily employed, maybe only for the reference week or for seasonal work; yet they are considered employed and in the same category as people with permanent jobs.

On the other side, there is an "underground economy," where inherently illegal activities (such as drug dealing) or illegal operations of legal activities (such as cleaning services or child-care providers working for cash undeclared as income in tax returns) take place. The people engaged in these activities are economically employed, but (for obvious reasons) are likely to be reported as unemployed by themselves or their household. If the workers involved were counted as employed, the unemployment figure would be lower—at least for that reason.

The most obvious change to the official unemployment figure, which would make it both higher and more realistic, would be to count as unemployed the discouraged workers who have given up looking for a job because they have tried unsuccessfully for so long. The government could certainly make this change, if it chose to do so. Obviously, it would be politically difficult to have a sudden jump in the unemployment figure just because of a more logical statistical count. But the BLS is supposed to be a nonpartisan branch of government. So it is unclear to me why it refuses to make this logical change in its count of the unemployed. Maybe the political problem could be evaded by making the change while in between Washington administrations.

Q What is an economically healthy and acceptable unemployment percentage?

A If the unemployment rate is continuously below the economically healthy level, the result would be runaway inflation, or higher and higher prices. Workers would realize that jobs were plentiful, and firms would pay higher and higher wages in order to fill the jobs. If the unemployment rate is continuously above the economically healthy level, there would be runaway deflation. With a shortage of jobs, workers would accept lower and lower wages in order to to keep their jobs. Lower and lower prices would result. So the economically healthy unemployment rate is associated with neither runaway inflation nor runaway deflation. Economists call that hypothetical unemployment rate (or something like it) the "natural rate of unemployment."

What is the natural rate of unemployment? Some economists think that the natural rate of unemployment is about 5 percent in the U.S. economy, but that it changes over time. One thing that can make it change is demographics. For example, younger workers change jobs more frequently than older workers and are obviously unemployed while in between jobs. So if the working population gets younger, the natural unemployment rate increases. Another influence on the natural rate is government policy. If the government establishes a high minimum wage, then more workers will try to get jobs but be unsuccessful, because firms will hire fewer workers at the higher pay—and again the natural unemployment rate will go up.

One way to estimate the natural rate of unemployment is to use the fact that employed workers are needed to produce goods and services (called "output"). Consider the total output of the economy. Gross domestic product (GDP) is the total output of the economy measured in dollars. Let's do two things to GDP as it moves—year by year over time. First, let's correct GDP for inflation to get "real GDP." (For example, if GDP increases by 5 percent in one year compared to the previous year and inflation is 3 percent, then real GDP went up by only about 2 percent.) Second, let's take the *trend growth* in real GDP ("trend real GDP"). This means that the business cycle ups and downs of real GDP are averaged out over time, resulting in a nice steady increase in real GDP. The unemployment rate associated with trend real GDP is an estimate of the natural rate of unemployment.

Chapter 3

PERSONAL FINANCE (YOUR MONEY)

It is safe to say that everyone wants to make a lot of money on their investments. It would be nice if economics could tell you how to do so really quickly. But reality intrudes—and *Everyday Economics* deals with reality, not fantasy. The advice given in this chapter is to save and invest for specific objectives, ideally for the long term. Also, beware of anyone who suggests a way of making a quick profit by placing your money in an investment you had not considered. As the saying goes, "if it is too good to be true, it isn't true."

○ Can I outguess the market?

△ No doubt you mean the stock market or any financial market. Unfortunately, the answer is "probably not." The fact that you can't outguess the market is illustrated in the following humorous anecdote, often told by economists to economists, and is expressed beautifully via direct quotation.

> There is an old joke, widely told among economists, about an economist strolling down the street with a companion. They come upon a $100 bill lying on the ground, and as the companion reaches down to pick it up, the economist says, "Don't bother—if it were a genuine $100 bill, someone would have already picked it up." This [is a] humorous example of economic logic gone awry.*

The common economic lesson that is being lampooned here is that there is no point in buying the stock of a company that you hear about on TV or see on the Internet as having high earnings prospects—for example, buying the stock of a company that has discovered a new technology—because by the time that you get around to buying the stock it is too late. Others will have bought it and the price of the stock will have already skyrocketed to reflect the discovery. More generally, the price of a company's stock at all times reflects all available information about the company's expected earnings.

The storyteller suggests a problem with this lesson. The fallacy, if you could call it that, is that some individual or some financial institution must have already taken advantage of the new information. Whoever does that first—whether by inside information (illegal though that may be), superior processing of public information, speed of reaction, or just luck—can indeed make a profit (capital gain) by

---

*Andrew W. Lo, "Efficient Markets Hypothesis," in Steven N. Durlauf and Lawrence E. Blume, eds., *The New Palgrave Dictionary of Economics,* 2nd edition (Houndsmills and New York: Macmillan, 2008), p. 782. Reproduced with permission of Palgrave Macmillan.

buying the stock at the previously low price and selling it at the new high price. Anyone who buys the stock later is out of luck. In terms of the anecdote, whoever picks up the $100 bill first will make a profit of $100; but there are no further *real* $100 bills to be picked up.

How can I be sure I have a comfortable retirement?

One issue here is what a comfortable retirement means. A comfortable retirement for a middle-class person would be much too low to suit a wealthy individual. We can think of a comfortable retirement as having sufficient recurring (say, annual) funds so that you can maintain the living standard to which you are accustomed. What percent of your income is that? It has to be less than 100 percent, because you now have certain expenses specific to work that you would not incur in retirement—special clothing, transportation, and pension contributions, for example. Also, at a lower level of income, your income taxes are likely to be lower. Perhaps 80 percent of previous gross (pretax, pre-other deductions) income is a good target.

So, for a comfortable retirement, you'll need a sufficiently high retirement income. Some decisions that you may be able to make to assure that are as follows:

1. *Work as long as you can so long as your health and happiness are not adversely affected.* The longer you work, the higher your retirement income will be, for two reasons. First, you will be contributing more to your retirement funding (via pension plans and savings). Second, you will have fewer retirement years to be financed.
2. *Retirement advisors advocate a three-leg approach to financing retirement: your employer's pension plan, social security, and your own savings.*
   a. Try to identify and work for a firm that has a good pension plan (although this is getting more and more difficult to find, as firms have been shifting from traditional pension

plans to employee savings plans). There are two main types of retirement plans: defined benefit and defined contribution. Under *defined benefit*, the amount of your pension is determined by formula, based on wages and years of service. The funding risk is borne by the firm, and the company is responsible for investing pension contributions made by the worker and firm. Under *defined contribution*, both employer and worker make contributions to a fund chosen by the worker (from a variety of alternatives arranged by the employer). The risk of bad investment and of consequent insufficient funds as planned for retirement is borne by the worker (employee), not the firm (employer). The firm makes its contributions to the pension fund, and that is all.

Because you will have your own savings and therefore are bearing investment risk for those funds, it's logical that (if all else is equal) you prefer a defined-benefit over a defined-contribution plan. Another reason is that the federal government, via its Pension Benefit Guaranty Corporation, guarantees pension benefits (though only up to a maximum amount) under a defined-benefit plan but not under a defined-contribution plan. Usually, you have no choice in the matter; but it is certainly a good idea to learn everything about a prospective employer's pension plan (and other benefits, especially health insurance) before you accept a job offer. A young person may never inquire about employers' pension plans. (Disclosure: I behaved that stupidly when I was young, too). But that is short-sighted. Benefits should enter into your employment decision as much as salary, commissions, and bonuses.

b. Know your retirement benefits under social security. Almost all American workers are eligible for social security retirement benefits. An important decision is when to begin your benefits. Some people do not understand that you have a right to social security retirement benefits even if you are still working. However, the longer you wait (up to age 70), the higher your retirement benefits. If you expect to live a long time, then it may pay to wait until 70 to collect your benefits. Complications exist when you receive a pension from certain employment not covered by social security and also when other family members (spouses and children) are involved. In particular, the pensions (but not wages) that people receive from some employers are reduced in the light of social security retirement benefits. That is one reason why it may be rational for these people to elect to begin receiving social security retirement benefits while working. Finally, Social Security advises that it may be to your benefit to begin receiving benefits in the month of January. In general, I have found it informative to consult the Social Security Web site and to speak to Social Security representatives.

c. Your own savings should be at least sufficient to assure you of enough retirement income, given your expected pension from your employer's pension plan and social security. Also, the more you save, the more likely you are to be able to finance a comfortable retirement earlier than you envisioned.

How should you invest your savings in order to reach your retirement objective? The general rule is that, the younger you are, the higher the proportion of your savings that should be allocated to stocks. As you grow older, the proportion allocated to bonds should increase at the expense of stocks. Some people do not follow that rule; rather, they keep a constant proportion of their portfolio in stocks—and they may be doing the right thing if their concern is an estate for future generations (children and grandchildren, or an ongoing charity). Some financial advisors have a corollary rule: the percentage of your investment (your accumulated investment, not just your savings for the current year) allocated to bonds should equal your age. So, for example, a 45-year-old person would have 45 percent of his retirement-oriented investment in bonds. My alternative rule is that if you invest steadily over time during your working years and cash out steadily over time during your retirement years, then you can have the benefit of the higher return of stocks over bonds while compensating for the greater risk of stocks.

3. *Adequate medical insurance is vital at all ages, and especially in retirement.* Know the cost and coverage of your employer's medical plan both while you are working and in retirement. Always opt for Medicare Part A (hospital insurance)—it is free when you turn 65. However, you will have to apply for Medicare Part A—you don't get it automatically. Other components of Medicare—Parts B (medical insurance covering physician services, outpatient care, and other items); D (prescription drug coverage); and C (private-company health plans approved by Medicare, incorporating both Parts A and B)—are not free, but could be important to you, depending on your own situation. Consider carefully when and whether to sign up for Medicare Part B and Medicare Part D. Those decisions should be coordinated with the rules of your employer's health plan. I recommend being very careful to do thorough research before electing Medicare Part C. The offerings of private companies may not have the permanence of Medicare itself, and that could be inconvenient to you.

Q If the stock market has been trending up since its inception, why do its setbacks seem to ruin people so dramatically? Also, would buying a wide variety of stocks reduce this bad effect?

A Yes, the stock market has an upward trend; but it is also extremely volatile. If an investor cashes in stocks at an inopportune time, that is, when the market is really down (a "bear market," or, worst case scenario, at the bottom of the bear market), he could indeed be ruined in the sense that a substantial portion of his equity (the value of his stocks) could go down the drain. The good news is that if stocks are sold when the market is really high (a "bull market," or, best case scenario, at the top of the bull market), then the person's wealth could increase substantially, and perhaps even double or triple.

On average, the market goes up: that is what the upward trend means. But the average means nothing to someone who must sell his stocks at a certain time in life, which unfortunately may happen to coincide with a bear market.

Let's shelve for the moment advice on how to counter the dilemma of bear markets happening at the wrong time and consider another danger, which the second part of the question addresses. If you own just one or even a few stocks, these stocks could go down even if the overall market goes up! To avoid that problem, you should diversify your stock holdings. Have a lot of different stocks in different sectors of the economy in your portfolio. In fact, you can even buy foreign stocks. While foreign stocks carry with them an exchange-rate risk (on the downside, they could be cashed in when the value of the dollar is unusually high, meaning the value of the foreign currency is very low) there is also an obvious upside in that they can provide substantial diversification.

What's the best way to diversify? The very best way is to be so wealthy that you can diversify on your own. Why? Because then you could hold the stocks until you needed the cash to buy a home, or to pay for your child's college education, or for some other expenditure requiring a lot of money. Unfortunately, few of us are so wealthy that we can do that.

The second best way to diversify is by purchasing shares in a mutual fund. At first glance, mutual funds seem to accomplish the objective in the same way that wealthy persons invest on their own. But no—a mutual fund is only a "second best." There are four reasons why this is the case. First, a mutual fund has expenses—office space, staff, and so on—and you, the investor in the fund, pay for that. Second, the mutual fund makes a profit, which you also pay for (even though this profit may be included in "expenses" or "fees"). Third, and most important, the mutual fund is typically "managed." What does that mean? It means that, instead of following the rule of simply buying and holding stocks until needed by its investors for cash, the fund buys and sells stocks in an attempt to "outperform the market." On average, the market cannot be outperformed. So, unless the fund is lucky or its managers are unusually skilled (which likely could be true only for brief time periods), managing a mutual fund of stocks simply adds to expenses—which you, the investor, must pay. Fourth, the fund can generate taxable capital gains for you, even though you yourself did not cash in shares. This is due to major unanticipated withdrawals from the fund, which typically happen during a bear market. The fund has to generate cash and cashes in some stocks at higher prices than it bought them—that is the meaning of capital gain.

Bottom line: Unless you are wealthy, the only way to diversify is to buy shares in a mutual fund. Try to pick one that is managed as little as you can decipher. Consider your investment in the mutual fund like paying taxes: You don't like it, but you have to do it. Buying mutual funds is the worst way to invest in stocks, except for all others! Also, try to save as much as you can, as early as you can. You may be pleasantly surprised at how much your money can grow over many years—providing you invest wisely and (admittedly) have a certain amount of luck in that respect.

Let's return to the bear market. How can you avoid the bad coincidence of such a market when you need money from the stocks (meaning shares in the mutual fund)? One way to avoid it is to time your decision to cash in stocks so that you are in a bull market, or at least only a little way into a bear market. If the purpose of the cash is to finance something that is not extremely time-sensitive, such as retirement or a down payment on a home, it may be possible to do that with only a little inconvenience. However, if the purpose is to finance something like a child's education, which is extremely time-sensitive, that may not be possible. You may have to bite the bullet.

There is one general way to assure that a bear market does not get you: Average your investments (buying stocks) and disinvestments (cashing in stocks) over time. The best way to invest in the stock market (via a mutual fund) is, month by month, to invest the same amount after correcting for inflation—so that you begin to invest more as your wages go up and as inflation increases. Be sure to take the cash out (sell your mutual fund shares) in the same way: in equal, inflation-corrected amounts month after month. If the time periods of your investment and disinvestment are both long enough, then your buying and selling in bull and bear markets will average out.

Most people don't do this. They want to "beat the market." They want to buy low and sell high. You are entitled to choose to try to do so. But then the market may beat you.

Q Are bonds a safer way to invest during an economic downturn?

A During an economic downturn, typically the stock market is also down. This is a good time to buy stocks—following the dictum, buy low—but many investors panic and sell stocks instead. Interest rates on the safest bonds are typically low during an economic downturn, as investors seek a safe haven by purchasing such bonds, thus bidding up their price. The safest bonds, from the standpoint of zero default risk (there is no chance of the bond-issuer not paying interest and principal) as well as low market risk (the market price would not fluctuate much until maturity, with little loss if the bond were sold in the market, prior to maturity) are short-term government securities. Therefore, because many investors are afraid of the stock market continuing to go down, they buy these securities at a high price and low yield, with little chance of further gain. But stocks, low in price, have a high probability of going up—providing one is patient enough to hold on to them. In a downturn, it is better to buy stocks rather than bonds—but, for most people, fear wins out over rationality.

Many friends and acquaintances solicit my investment advice during a recession and/or when the stock market is down. I always suggest that they certainly not sell their stocks—and indeed that they buy stocks, providing they have extra cash. Sometimes they even follow my advice.

Q What is the best way to try to rebuild an investment portfolio after a major drop in the market? Also, should I sell during an up-market— and, if so, what should I do with the funds?

A The stock market is best approached as a major part of your long-term investment. To try to achieve short-term capital gains (selling at higher prices than you buy) could just as well result in short-term capital losses. Normally, I advocate a "buy-and-hold" strategy for stock-market investment—withdrawing only when a major expenditure is needed, and preferably over a long period of time, not all at once.

Your first question has an obvious answer: Do nothing. If you have held on to your stock portfolio, then you still have the same stocks and in the same amounts as before the drop in the market. You have exactly the same ownership share of the corporations behind the stocks as you did before the down market. All that has happened is that each of your shares has a lower valuation than before. Eventually the market will go up, and—if there is nothing specific about your particular stocks that give them a permanently low market valuation—so will your stocks. That is, the valuation of your stocks will return, and even surpass, where they were before. Patience and courage are required when the market is down.

Some financial advisors might say that a down market is a good time to evaluate your investment portfolio and see if there is any reason to reallocate its components. For example, they might recommend more or less stocks relative to bonds. My own view is that you should regularly review your portfolio as you go through life. As your age, family status, and earning power change, so might the components of your investment portfolio. Major changes in financial markets and the real economy might also lead you to do that; but I worry about you doing it during a down market, because you might be prone to sell your stocks out of fear rather than looking at the long term.

My answer to the second question is related to the first. Selling stock during an up-market could be very profitable, providing you sell at a sufficiently high price compared to the price at which you bought the stocks. But did you buy at a low enough price? And can you time your selling at a high enough price? Ideally, you want to buy at the bottom of the market and sell at the top. Can you come close to doing that, when everyone else is trying to do the same thing?

Obviously, if you are going to sell short term, you should sell when the market is up. But, if the market continues to go up, then you will regret (both emotionally as well as financially) that you sold too soon. If you expect that the market will continue to go up, then the funds should be placed back in the market! At that point, of course, you should not have sold in the first place. And that's the problem with approaching the market as a source of short-term gain: You can buy with the intention of selling when the market goes up, or goes up more compared to when you bought, but the market may not have gone up, or gone up enough, when you intend to sell.

If you were clairvoyant, if you could predict the future of the stock market, you would treat the stock market as a source of short-term capital gains. You would sell at the top of the market and park the proceeds in an absolutely secure asset: Federal Deposit Insurance Corporation (FDIC)–insured deposits at a financial institution. The expected return (interest) would be low compared to other assets, but there could be no loss of principal. Then, when the market hits bottom, you would cash in your deposits and buy stocks again. Buy low and sell high, buy low and sell high—a great strategy, if only you knew when to buy and when to sell.

There are those who claim to know when to buy and when to sell so that capital gains are assured. These people—who could be friends of yours or could be managers of mutual funds—can point to their experience of making money in the stock market. How did they make money, unless they knew when to buy and when to sell? When the market is booming, anyone can make money by buying at an earlier time and selling at a later time. But sometimes "later" is too late; it is after the market has gone down. Imagine that the market goes down a bit and you continue to hold, thinking it's just a temporary movement. Imagine that this is the start of a crash. You plan to sell the "next day," but you're too late, and you sell at a loss.

If you want "technical" advice on how to play the market, with the objective of short-term capital gains, you would have to get the advice from someone else. However, I urge you to be very careful of adopting any investment strategy advocated by someone who claims to know how to "beat the market."

Disclaimer: In general, this advice carries with it my own views on how to make investments. Reasonable people could have other views. Also, if you are lucky enough to be wealthy, any change in your investment portfolio could have serious tax implications. Whatever advice I give needs to be tempered, and, if necessary, altered or even rejected, if your tax situation is affected. Because people are in different tax brackets and have different portfolios, each situation could be different. Any major event affecting a large investment portfolio could benefit from professional tax advice—which is not my expertise. So my advice can be only general and without reference to taxes.

Q Why shouldn't I just keep my money in a savings account?

A The reason not to do so is given by virtually all financial advisors. Although you would have ultimate safety (assuming that your account is fully insured), you would get low return. It would be most unwise to keep your entire portfolio in bank accounts. You want more earning power, especially if you are saving for a long-term purpose such as retirement. Stock (mutual) funds and bond funds have much higher expected returns than bank deposits, albeit with more risk, and certainly the former should be an important part of your portfolio (unless you are already retired).

There are four keys to a sound investment strategy. First, be concerned with specific objectives: funds for retirement, for a home, or for college for your children. Second, the objectives should be as long-term as possible—this means that you save early and as much as you can before you cash in any part of your investments. Third, diversify. Don't put all of your funds in stocks or all in bonds or all in the bank. And diversify within stocks or bonds themselves by having a lot of different stocks and bonds. You probably will have to invest in mutual funds to accomplish the third objective. Fourth, change your diversification strategy as your own personal situation changes, meaning changes in your age, family status, earning power, and other sources of funds (such as inheritances).

Q If I have a standard savings account with a given bank, what legal protections exist for my money? What amount is absolutely guaranteed if the bank should declare bankruptcy?

A The first thing for you to do is to make sure that your bank is a member of the Federal Deposit Insurance Corporation (FDIC). This is extremely important, because the FDIC insures your deposits. If your bank is not a member, then your only recourse is the application of bankruptcy law. As a depositor in the bank, you are a creditor of the bank and so are entitled to recovery of your funds—but possibly only in part and certainly after a period of time—should the bank be liquidated and its assets sold to pay off its debts.

In general, it is unwise to have your checking and savings deposits in a bank that is not a FDIC member. The simplest way to check whether your bank is in fact a member is to see a conspicuous sign to that effect in your bank or to locate FDIC booklets on a counter in your bank. If it is unclear whether your bank is a FDIC member, ask the bank manager for proof. The surest way is to go to the FDIC Web site and search for your bank by name to ensure that it is a member institution. Members of the FDIC include not only commercial banks but also other "thrift institutions" (meaning they accept deposits). Only banks chartered by the federal government ("nationally chartered banks") are required to be members of the FDIC. Others may apply for membership. Obviously, a lot of banks and similar institutions voluntarily join the FDIC, because in that way they become more attractive to customers who want their deposits insured.

The FDIC insures deposits up to a certain amount, subject to rules. The amount of insurance per deposit category in a particular bank (or thrift institution) changes over time. In 2008 it was increased from $100,000 to $250,000—but the increase was supposed to be only temporary, ending after December 31, 2009. The amount limit (say, $250,000) applies to each type of account in each bank. One way to increase the amount insured is to create different account types or different account ownership within the same bank (single account, joint account, allowable retirement account). Another way is to have the same type of account at different banks. Be advised that the same type of account *at different branches* of the same bank counts as only one insured account.

The beauty of FDIC insurance is that it is automatic, with no application from the depositor required. Also, FDIC pays off quickly should the bank fail. The FDIC insurance for your accounts is absolutely guaranteed by the U.S. government, providing the bank is a member institution and providing you follow the rules to make sure all your accounts are insured in total. However, bear in mind that FDIC insurance applies only to certain assets: checking accounts, savings accounts, money-market deposit accounts, and certificates of deposits (CDs). Insurance does *not* apply to other types of investment (bonds, stocks, mutual funds, and so on), *even if arranged by the bank.* As for what is in your safety-deposit box, you are on your own; FDIC insurance does not apply.

How much debt is it okay to have?

The amount of debt that you can safely have depends on three things. First, if you are making an important and sound investment with the debt, then the debt might be okay. A home is the most important investment that middle-class families have. So it is okay to take out a mortgage in order to generate funds beyond your down payment for the purchase of a home. What is *not* okay is to take out a "home equity loan" on your home. That is a fancy term for a second mortgage. Many families have lost their homes by taking out "equity loans" that cannot be repaid. Your mortgage—by which I mean *your first and only mortgage*—should be as low as your financial circumstances permit. You do not want to take a chance on losing your home or your good credit standing.

I am very much in favor of a fixed-rate mortgage rather than a variable-rate mortgage. A low initial rate followed by a formula-driven later rate that depends on a market interest rate means that you, the borrower, bear the risk of what happens to interest rates in the future. You want the lender, the holder of your mortgage, to bear that risk, which a fixed-rate mortgage assures. *It is your responsibility to read the fine print of a mortgage (or any legal document) before you sign anything.* Further, I strongly advise that you have an attorney representing your interests present when you formally purchase or sell a home.

The second factor that determines the amount of debt you can safely carry is your future earning power. If your future income is likely to be low and is not expected to grow or is uncertain, then be very hesitant about taking on any debt whatsoever. The third factor is how important you view your (or your family's) future compared to your present standard of living. The more debt you have now, the lower your standard of living will be in the future, because you will be paying off the debt. A big exception is the education of your children. It is generally wise for you to borrow and for your children themselves to borrow for their college education or occupational training, because their future earning power will be enhanced.

ᵠ Should I be paying off my credit cards in full, or is it okay to carry a balance?

Ⓐ For almost all circumstances, I do not advocate carrying any credit-card debt whatsoever. To get into the habit of not having such debt, I suggest that your college-age children be allowed to have only a debit card rather than a credit card. Debit cards do not involve debt; monies spent are taken directly from a bank account.

The reason for this strict advice relates to the high interest and related charges that credit-card companies assess on unpaid balances. Better to obtain a conventional consumer loan from your local bank. Also, unless you are a disciplined person, credit-card debt gives you the opportunity to charge, charge, charge for purchases to enhance your standard of living. Some people then obtain cards from other credit-card companies and get further and further in debt. Eventually their "house of cards" comes tumbling down and they get into an awful financial and personal mess. It is easy to get into this mess with undisciplined credit-card spending, but hard to get out of the mess in an acceptable way.

▣ How can I tell if my broker is doing a good job?

Ⓐ My first comment is: Why have a broker? He has no special knowledge about specific investments and no inside information to guide you (and acting on inside information can get you into legal difficulty, in any event). Why pay for someone to give you advice that at best is common sense and at worst is counterproductive?

But if you must have a broker, then here are the warning signs:

1. *Beware of advice that involves too many transactions.* Do not trust a broker who advocates a lot of buying and selling of individual stocks. The market evaluates stocks better than your broker.

2. *Stocks and bonds, in particular, should be held for long-term objectives.* If your broker advises that you have the short-term objective of "beating the market," that is a bad sign concerning his competence to give sound investment advice.

3. *Examine carefully the fees or commissions that your broker charges for his own services or for third parties that are the source of his recommended investments for you.* If these fees are not low, you should be suspicious.

4. Finally, and most important: *If your broker gives you advice to buy or sell anything on short notice, don't do it—and drop your broker immediately.* Any investment involving a substantial sum of money (from your standpoint) should be made with thought and foresight.

Q Everyone tells me that I have to know where my 401(k) is invested, and I haven't the slightest clue or really the time to do the research. How is an average person with no financial training expected to make these difficult choices that will impact his retirement fund?

A A 401(k) is a retirement savings plan that has definite tax advantages. The offering of this plan is at the discretion of the employer. You are fortunate that your employer has such a plan, and you are wise to invest in it not only for the tax advantages but also for the matching funds that the typical firm provides to supplement your own contributions.

Usually the employee (you) has the job of selecting how to invest the funds among the investment alternatives that the plan offers. Most plans include one or more of several kinds of mutual funds: money market, stocks, bonds, and funds consisting of combinations of these three basic investments. Some plans include other options, including purchases of the firm's own stocks. If you do not make your own decision on how to allocate your savings and the matching contribution of your employer to these alternative investments, then it is probably done for you according to specified rules or formulas. That default allocation may seem perfectly beneficial for you, but it may be to your advantage to compare it with an allocation that you decide for yourself. Here are some basic rules that should enter into your own allocation decision.

1. *Contribute the maximum permitted by the 401(k) plan, provided that you can afford that maximum.* Otherwise, contribute

as much as you can afford. Such tax-advantage plans should be the first call for your savings for retirement. Per dollar invested, you will generate more dollars for your retirement in a tax-advantage investment than in alternatives without that characteristic.

2. *The younger you are, the greater the allocation you should make to stocks.* While stocks are riskier than bonds, they yield a higher return over the long run. As you get closer to retirement age, you should allocate more to bonds.

3. *The money-market fund typically has the least risky return, because the investments are very short-term (treasury bills, commercial paper), but it also has the lowest return.* Usually, that fund should be used only as a parking place for your savings while you are about to make an allocation decision. Also, the money-market fund would be a good place for amounts that you intend to withdraw in the near future. But you should be very cautious about any withdrawal at all, both because you lose some of the advantages of the 401(k) investment and because you can incur additional disadvantages (such as taxation). If you desperately need money, it is possible to borrow from your 401(k); but again there are rules, and they can be complex. You should receive competent advice before any withdrawal at all from the 401(k)— even for retirement itself. Also, be aware of the rules for compulsory withdrawal, which apply after you reach age 70½.

4. *Rules 2 and 3 should apply to all your savings, or rather to all your retirement-oriented savings.* If you are fortunate enough to have sufficient funds to save beyond your employer's retirement plan, then you should consider all your savings together for rules 2 and 3. The rules need not apply to each savings outlet separately, rather only in total. If you are even more fortunate to be independently wealthy or expect to receive a substantial inheritance, then you should consult a tax attorney or other expert for advice.

Q **If my 401(k) contribution is taxed upon withdrawal in however many years, or, as per the Roth 401(k), taxed up front but not upon withdrawal, how is it better than any other savings account? Also, what should I base my decision on with regard to whether to invest in a Roth (tax up front) 401(k) versus the standard 401(k)?**

A As you correctly state, the standard (also called "traditional") 401(k) has no income tax on the employee's contributions. That is, no matter how it is invested (within the plan), all earnings (interest, dividends, capital gains) are tax-free until withdrawal. However, the entirety of amounts withdrawn does enter your gross income and is subject to income tax.

The Roth 401(k) involves contributions from after-tax dollars. That appears to give all advantage to the traditional 401(k). However, providing special rules regarding a "qualified distribution" (meaning, qualified withdrawal) are followed, the amounts withdrawn do *not* enter your gross income and therefore are not subject to income tax. The rules for a "qualified distribution" are firm: You must have been in the plan for at least five years and be at least age 59½ or disabled.

The 59½-year requirement also applies to traditional 401(k) plans, with possible exceptions; otherwise, there is a tax penalty. Anyone desiring to make a withdrawal from either 401(k) plan under any circumstances (whether retirement, hardship, or other need for funds) should understand thoroughly the rules of the particular plan and consider whether an alternative source of funds would be more advantageous. One possibility might be for you to borrow from your own 401(k) plan; again, you should make an informed decision only after weighing the advantages and disadvantages (compared to those of alternatives) of withdrawal from a 401(k) plan.

In most situations, you generate more funds for retirement by opting for the traditional plan as opposed to the Roth 401(k). The reason for this is that your contributions are greater, as you do not have to deduct income tax before making them, as the Roth 401(k) requires.

So your 401(k) has a larger base to grow on over time. The fact that you have to pay taxes upon withdrawal generally is not enough of an off-set to overcome the advantage of pretax contributions.

The exception is if you expect to have a high income (from all sources, not just your 401(k) plan) in your retirement years. Then withdrawals from the traditional 401(k) could place you in a higher in-come-tax bracket, whereas withdrawals from a Roth plan would not do so. Even in that case, you may want to allocate your funds partly to a traditional and partly to a Roth plan. It should be noted that employ-ees can offer a traditional 401(k) without a Roth 401(k), but not the re-verse. So if your employee has only one 401(k) plan, you can be sure that it is the traditional one.

Q What should I do when my mortgage is transferred from one bank to another?

A You should continue to make your payments as billed to cover mortgage interest, mortgage principal, and real-estate tax. Your obli-gation as a borrower is to meet your obligations to pay back the debt. Your responsibility to do so is not affected by the fact that the holder of the mortgage is now another institution. On the other side, the new bank has no additional rights compared to the former bank. In par-ticular, the new bank cannot unilaterally alter the mortgage conditions unless permitted by the mortgage document. So the transfer of the mortgage should not affect you in any essential way.

Chapter 4

PERSONAL SPENDING (YOUR PURCHASES)

In this chapter, *Everyday Economics* offers you precise advice on how to spend your dollars on certain goods and services. You will find, for example, a discussion on the pros and cons of purchasing an extended warranty that will be of use to you time and again. Also, learning how to apply economics when you buy a new car or sell your used car could be worth thousands of dollars to you. Other types of questions and answers give you an understanding of the operation of markets in general.

Q Since there are so many uncertainties in life, shouldn't I enjoy my money while I am young?

A Many people do just that, especially when they are young. That kind of behavior means that your consumption of goods and services now means a lot more to you than your consumption of goods and services in the future. Economists would say that you have "a high rate of time preference"—you want things now rather than in the future. It doesn't mean that you are selfish; you might want to spend your money *now* on your family and friends or on charities.

As they grow older and acquire family responsibilities, many people change to a "lower rate of time preference." They become concerned about providing for the well-being of their entire family, not just in the present but also in the future. For example, they might start saving for their children's education or for the down payment on a home. Even a young person may become financially responsible for a parent or other relative. That could mean supporting the relative directly or managing the relative's savings.

So either a high or a low rate of time preference can be rational. In general, the extent of your desire to provide for the future depends on such factors as your age, extent of family obligation, and cultural environment.

Q Is it irrational to buy Bayer aspirin instead of much cheaper generic or store-brand aspirin? After all, the chemical composition of aspirin is the same, regardless of the manufacturer. Also, is it irrational to buy Coca-Cola or Pepsi-Cola at the higher price instead of an off-brand cola drink, which is essentially the same stuff but at a lower price?

A The two cases are not the same. Consider the cola drinks first. Coke and Pepsi are not quite the same drink, and each is slightly different from other cola drinks. There are differences in the ingredients, or at least the mix of the ingredients, in the various cola products. So the different cola drinks do have different tastes. On top of that, and very important for brand loyalty, is the fact that the top brands, including Coke and Pepsi, advertise heavily in favor of their own colas. This advertising predisposes some people to like the drinks, whether for taste or by stimulating their desire to emulate the beautiful people who appear drinking Coke or Pepsi in advertisements, commercials, and billboards.

Aspirin is another, more complicated, case. It is true that aspirin is aspirin—there is only one way to make it. So why do people buy Bayer, paying more for the same product? The answer is that people are judging quality by price. Bayer charges a higher price, so people assume that it must be a better product. Also, we again have the influence of advertising. Bayer advertises, whereas the generic brand does not; any advertising done by the store brand is much less than Bayer. Some customers are moved by the thought of quality control: Aspirin is a drug, and they want to be sure that they are getting the correct mix of ingredients and the precise dosage that is stated on the package. Bayer is a well-known company, and therefore is viewed as the least likely manufacturer to make a mistake in its product. It is probably true that the quality control in the generic or store-brand aspirin is just as good as Bayer—but the customer has no way of finding this out. So some people buy Bayer, the number-one advertised and most popular brand.

Bottom line: It is rational to make your economic decisions not only on price but also on other factors that are important to you. It is also rational to do the opposite and decide that you will buy only the cheapest brand. Economics does not say that only one possible decision is rational.

Q Should I buy an extended warranty when I purchase a durable good, such as a refrigerator, television set, personal computer, or other appliances?

A The typical answer given by consumer advisors is that, as a general rule, you should not purchase an extended warranty. The reason is that manufacturers would not offer the extended warranty unless it was profitable for them to do so and, therefore, purchasing the warranty is to the consumer's disadvantage. Sometimes the general rule is amended by acknowledging that if you, like many consumers, are "risk averse" and are concerned about the consequences of the product failing, then you should consider buying the extended warranty.

Economics tells us that, *whether or not the general rule is valid,* the reason for the rule is incorrect! Private economic transactions—such as those between a consumer and manufacturer (with the retailer as intermediary)—are voluntary and these types of transactions should benefit both parties. For example, suppose I buy a bicycle from you. The normal outcome is *both* that I pay less money than the bicycle is worth to me, *and* that you receive more money than the bicycle is worth to you. The same logic applies to the extended warranty. Granted, the manufacturer would not offer this warranty unless it expects to make a profit. But you, the purchaser of the product, could nevertheless benefit from buying the warranty.

Economics can help consumers in good (what economists call "rational") decision-making. In the situation at hand, elements entering into the decision include: (1) the probability of the product failing (or, more generally, requiring repair for good functioning); (2) the cost of replacing the product (in the event that the product is defective and either cannot be fixed or you decide will not be repaired); (3) the cost of the warranty; and (4) the extent of your willingness to accept the inconvenience of arranging for a third party to repair the product as well as the uncertain cost of third-party repair. Consider these elements in turn.

1. *The higher the probability of the product failing, the more rational it is to purchase the extended warranty.* Usually, one would assign a high probability of failure to products new on the market and, to a lesser extent, to radically new versions of existing products. Flat-panel television sets fall into one or the other of these categories. Recently I did decide to purchase an extended warranty for my new model flat-panel TV. But

sometimes even existing products might have a high failure rate. For example, again as a consumer, I have had conversations with repairpersons of refrigerators (definitely an old product). These conversations suggest that certain vital components of new refrigerators tend to have a high failure rate after a few years. I trust the repairpersons, and so, as a matter of course, I purchased an extended warranty for a new refrigerator and benefited when two components were replaced under warranty free of charge. This was done on two separate occasions.

So it is up to you to do the research: speak to objective people (friends, repairpersons) involved in the product. (Obviously, the views of salespersons and manufacturers may be less trustworthy, because they have an interest in selling you the product and the warranty.) Also, consumer magazines may help provide information on specific products. If your research finds that the new or even existing product that you want to buy seems to have problems and you don't want to wait for the next generation of products, it makes sense to buy the warranty.

2. *The higher the cost of replacing the product, the more rational it is to buy the extended warranty.* Note that what is relevant is the cost of replacement, not the cost of the original purchase. The latter cost is a "sunk cost," and a fundamental rule of rational decision making is that sunk costs are irrelevant. So if you expect the price of the product to fall over time (*not* how much you originally paid), it doesn't make sense to buy a warranty. One product category that clearly falls in price is computers.

3. *Obviously, if the extended warranty costs very little* compared to the cost of repurchasing the product or compared to the cost of a third-party repair, *then there is a strong case in favor of the warranty.*

4. *If you are fearful of the consequences of doing without the product for an uncertain period of time, reluctant to experience the hassle of arranging for third-party repair, or unhappy with an*

uncertain cost of third-party repair, these concerns would lead you to buy the extended warranty—and that would be a rational decision.

My computer-guru friends tell me that newly purchased personal computers tend to fail during the first year (some say, even the first month) *or not at all,* and they advise me *not* to buy an extended warranty. But, for me, the consequences of working without a computer beyond one day would be devastating. Therefore the gurus understand my decision to purchase a one-day service extended warranty for a new computer and renew the warranty as long as the manufacturer permits. Getting the warranty is a rational decision for me—sometimes it's just personal security that is the motivator!

In addition, the duration and fine print of the warranty obviously will enter into your decision. Before even beginning to consider the above four points, you need to understand which parts of the product are covered and for how long, how to arrange for a repair, how long the repair will take, and whether there will be a replacement product if repair is not possible. If these points are not clear in writing, forget about the warranty and perhaps forget about buying the product itself.

Q What advice can economics give me about buying a new car?

A The most important fact about buying a new car is that it is a process of bargaining, or negotiation. Buying a car is not the same as going grocery shopping. The price of a given model car varies from buyer to buyer. Obviously, you want to pay the lowest possible price for the car that you buy. The problem is that the salesperson and the new-car manager are much better bargainers than you and me. They have training in negotiating skills that we don't have and they have a lot more experience negotiating than we have. Also, they work together as a team, so their bargaining advantage is multiplied.

You have to build up your negotiating power so that you are not put at a serious disadvantage. Here is some important information. First, do not worry about getting a "lemon" when you buy a new car. Quality control in automobile manufacturing has improved significantly in recent years, both for U.S.-based and overseas production. While there are still some horror stories of consumers being stuck with lemons, the chance of you being one of them is so low that you should not devote any mental energy to that issue. Rather, learn how to bargain effectively.

Second, understand that one feature of how the automobile market works is to your advantage in bargaining. Dealers purchase and prepay for automobiles from the manufacturer. Sometimes dealers use their own cash; sometimes they borrow money to make this payment. Either way, the automobiles on the dealers' lots are costing money, or have cost money, and will not bring in any revenue until they are sold. Therefore *the dealer wants to sell cars as soon as possible.* If you are perceived as a serious customer, meaning someone who wants to buy a car that day, you are a desirable person to have in the dealer's showroom. So do not be timid—walk proud.

Third, there is a bargaining paradox that fascinates economists and that you must appreciate to get a good deal. *It is essential that you conceal your true feelings toward a particular vehicle.* If the salesperson perceives that you really want a particular car, up goes the price. In a bargaining situation, it is sometimes important to bluff the opposite of what you believe.

Fourth, you may have heard about a field of study called "neuroscience" or "neuroeconomics," which looks at consumer decisions (such as buying a car) as a neurological phenomenon. Do not worry about that. It is extremely unlikely that the salesperson and manager are knowledgeable in the field. In any event, neuroscience or neuroeconomics is not thought control. Be secure applying the bargaining tips that are presented here.

Fifth, rather than preparing for your car shopping expedition by deciding on one particular model car, try to look at a car the way economists look at a car. "A car is not a car. It is a bundle of characteristics."

Look at any car as a combination of style, safety, gas-mileage performance, roominess, and so on. Once you do this, you can then rank the attributes in importance and be prepared to trade off among them. Why is this mental shift from specific model to bundle of characteristics important? Because, to get the lowest price on a car, you must not "fall in love" with a particular model. Rather, your philosophy should be that any car is nothing but a bundle of attributes.

Then, I suggest the following step-by-step procedure:

1. *Find several (at least three) different models of cars in your price range that have an acceptable combination of the characteristics that you like.* For this information, go to consumer-oriented Web sites or to print consumer magazines. For the moment, accept the price range given in the sources that you consult. It is important to select several cars—preferably at least three—that fit your needs in characteristics and in price. The cars on your list should be from more than one manufacturer, and it is absolutely essential that the cars be sold by more than one dealer. You should select at least three different dealers.

2. *Add optional equipment only as needed to fulfill your characteristics preference—and do not go beyond that preference.* In general, when a feature is standard, that is, included in the base model, you will pay less for it than when it is an add-on. However, sometimes going down to a cheaper model and adding on some equipment is more cost effective than staying with a more expensive model that includes unnecessary extra equipment to satisfy your characteristics preference. (Sometimes options are offered only in a certain combination rather than singly.) So you may want to try the pricing both ways before moving to the next step.

3. *For each of your selected models, get the dealer invoice price, which is essentially the dealer's wholesale price.* Do that for the base model plus for each of the options chosen. Also obtain the manufacturer's "holdback" for the vehicle. The holdback is a rebate that the manufacturer gives the dealer after the car is

sold. It is a specified percentage of the invoice price. Finally, obtain the dealer incentives, if any. This is an amount, in addition to the holdback, that the manufacturer provides to the dealer for selling certain models. You may have to pay a consumer-oriented service for this information. Do so. *Do not even think about buying a new car without having all this information for all your alternative models.* Obviously, the information must be timely. It can change; so get the info shortly before you decide to visit dealers.

4. *You will be visiting several dealerships, because you have several alternative models to consider.* It is a good idea to bring another person with you to the dealership, preferably a relative or close friend who has your interests well at heart. Then, psychologically, the salesperson and manager know that they have to satisfy two people, not one.

5. *Your first action should be to visit each dealership and request a test-drive of the vehicle, preferably without the salesperson or other dealer employee present, but definitely with your relative or friend in the car.* If the test-drive indicates that the car is not to your satisfaction, walk out, no matter what the salesperson says to you. So now you have test-driven all the models that satisfy your preferences. Then visit each dealership again and begin the negotiation process.

6. *Negotiate up rather than down.* You know the dealer's full and true cost of the vehicle. Begin with an offer that gives the dealer a modest profit (including holdback and dealer incentives)—perhaps no more than $800—and make the salesperson and/or manager work hard to persuade you to pay more. If the price becomes too high in your mind, begin to get up from your seat *slowly.* If you are obviously a serious buyer, the salesperson will call you back. If not, walk out and do not return. Always remember that you have alternatives.

7. *Your objective is to obtain a written offer from the dealer, effective for a brief but reasonable period of time, perhaps 24 hours.* You must make sure that the offer is the "walk-away price."

Use that term with the salesperson. "Walk-away price" means the offer should include *everything,* even taxes. It is the amount of the check that you will write to pay for the car. (By the way, along with some consumer advisory services, I do *not* recommend purchasing an extended warranty for a new-car purchase.)

8. *Never write the check or obtain financing the same day.* Impulse purchases and impulse financing are inadvisable for a big-ticket item—and, for most of us, an automobile is a big-ticket item. Go home and mull over any offers and discuss them with your spouse, other relative, or close friend. Compare the offers and choose the one that either is cheapest or has the highest ratio of desired characteristics to price.

9. *Avoid trading in your used car.* You will do much better selling it privately or to another dealer separately. Also avoid financing your car via the dealership. You are probably better off obtaining financing separately. Allowing the salesperson and manager to combine car, trade-in, and financing makes the negotiations complicated for you but not for them. Do not give them any advantage. Keep things simple; follow your plan. If feasible, buy the car with cash. (On a personal note, I never buy a car that I cannot purchase in cash.) Once you have the opportunity of obtaining credit, the salesperson and manager know that you have the means of paying a higher price than otherwise. That increases their negotiating strength; and, believe me, their negotiating skills are high enough as it is.

How should I go about buying a used car or selling my used car?

A lot of advice on buying and selling used cars is provided by consumer-oriented organizations, and much of the advice is worthwhile. But these organizations fail to emphasize the most important economic fact about transacting in a used car—and this fact applies whether you buy or sell: The information about the specific car being transacted is one-sided. The seller always has the particular information about the car's condition; the buyer does not. The seller always knows whether or not the car is a "lemon," but the buyer does not know whether or not it is a lemon.

You might think that the one-sidedness of information gives the advantage to the seller of the car. But in fact that is not the case. Why not? Because the buyer's lack of the seller's information makes the buyer wary. To avoid overpaying for a bad vehicle that will perform much worse than its appearance suggests, the buyer will assume that the vehicle is a lemon and pay no more than that would entail—even if the car is in fact well-maintained and in all respects a great vehicle.

How do you get around this problem? The consumer organizations suggest that you acquire information. Do the research. Go on the Internet. Find out the "book value" of the vehicle in question, find out the price at which used-car dealers are buying or selling the vehicle. The organizations also recommend that you make your car look good and do repairs. And that you have a mechanic check out a used car that you intend to buy.

Not all of this advice makes sense, especially if you are selling the car. Sprucing up an obviously old car so that it looks new could be a mistake. Why? Because the one-sidedness of information makes the prospective purchaser nervous to begin with. If the car looks too good, a potential buyer could become even more suspicious that your car is a "disguised lemon."

You can get around this by full disclosure. How can the buyer of your car be absolutely sure that your car is not a lemon? When the buyer is the place where you have your car serviced. Then the buyer has the record of the entire maintenance and repair history of your car. After all, the buyer—usually the dealer from whom you bought the car when new—is the very entity that has kept your car in good shape. Several years ago, following my own advice, I sold my used car to the dealer from whom I originally bought the car. I began by asking to see the used-car manager. He asked permission to examine the car for a few hours, and I said: "Of course; take as long as you want." The price that I received was about double what I expected, and the manager actually apologized that he could not offer more, because the car was in such good shape!

This experience suggests that if you choose not to sell your car where it was maintained and repaired (or if that place does not buy used cars), then at least get all records from the place where you did get the car maintained and repaired. Make copies of the records for the prospective purchasers of your car.

When you are on the other side of the transaction (the buyer), you should try to obtain the same information: the maintenance and repair record of the car. Of course, the record that you get may not be complete. But at least it is something. Also, unlike when you buy a new car, *purchasing any warranty should be seriously considered when you buy a used car.*

◎ Is eBay an example of fair market price? Should all products be sold via an auction model?

🅰 The word "fair" is difficult to interpret, as your idea of what is "fair" could be different from my idea. A logical interpretation of "fair market price" is that you mean the price that would be established by demand and supply under competitive conditions. That would require a large number of buyers, a large number of sellers, a homogenous product, and perfect information known to all. The resulting price is called "the competitive price."

The eBay auction model does not fit these conditions. There is not a large number of sellers of any specific item, and there is not necessarily a large number of buyers of the item. If a variety of items in the same product category is up for auction, it is very unlikely that the items are identical—if only because of differing quality, both inherently (a new, unused item) and in terms of use and obsolescence (if the item is used). Also, the auction approach lends itself to "gaming" strategies and possible collusion among prospective buyers, although eBay claims to have safeguards to prevent this type of behavior.

There is a type of auction that would fit the economist's idea of a competitive market and would result in a competitive price. That would be when the auctioneer begins by announcing a particular price. Each market participant then declares how much (in physical terms, not in dollar amount) of the product she would either buy at that price or sell at that price. If the amount that would be bought exceeds the amount that would be sold, the auctioneer raises the price and repeats the process. If the amount that would be sold exceeds the amount that would be bought, the auctioneer lowers the price and repeats the process. Eventually there is a price at which the amount that would be sold exactly equals the amount that would be bought. That is the competitive price. Note that no transactions would occur until the competitive price is determined.

The eBay auction can be of various types and have specific rules, but the auction is definitely not like that described above. So it is unlikely that eBay auctions result in the competitive price for any item. Indeed, when an item sold is unique, the economist's competitive model has no applicability. With only one seller and no good substitute product available elsewhere, the market power of the seller becomes paramount ("buy from me, or you can't get the product at all"). If combined with only a few prospective buyers, the element of bargaining—decidedly not a characteristic of the competitive model—comes to the front. Under an auction, the bargaining takes the form of a minimum bid set by the seller and decisions on bidding made by the buyers. Also, the information released by the eBay auction model as the auction proceeds is incomplete and partly misleading. The eBay auction model is not the same as an open auction, in which bids are publicly and exactly known to all auction participants.

So, no, economists would not advocate that all products be sold via an auction model—not if the norm is a competitive model. Having said that, the good of e-commerce firms such as eBay must also be recognized. Economic transactions over the Internet constitute one of the remarkable innovations of the computer age. Not only consumer–business but also business–business transactions increasingly take place via the Internet. The Internet "perfects the market"; that is, in many ways it brings market results closer to the competitive ideal. The cost to consumers of looking for the best price of a given product is very low, and it is a time-and-effort cost only; compared to the time, effort, *and* money costs of traveling from store to store or even telephoning the stores to obtain the product information. The same applies to searching for the highest-quality product for a given price.

Also, the Internet makes it easy for consumers to switch from one seller to another, and easy for businesses to advertise and change prices and items offered for sale. Payment can be made over the Internet, using credit or debit cards directly, or via PayPal (itself owned by eBay). It is easy for businesses to assemble sales data and for consumers to share feedback on products, sometimes via the businesses themselves, sometimes via intermediaries such as eBay. When the product is itself purely digital (music, video, computer programs, information, access to e-books, and so on), it is even supplied via the Internet. It is a fair statement that the role of the Internet in reducing shopping costs, transportation costs, and transactions costs in general adds much more to economic efficiency than does any Internet-based auction model.

How can airlines charge such different fares for the same round-trip? Isn't this an unfair pricing practice?

Yes, it certainly seems unfair that the same airplane trip can cost different people wildly different amounts. If your ticket is refundable rather than nonrefundable, it costs more. If you buy the ticket in advance or are lucky enough to find a last-minute cheap seat, your ticket costs less. If you stay over a Saturday night, it can also cost less. The price of the ticket between the same two airports can vary with day of travel, time of travel (over the 24-hour day), date of travel (weekday or weekend, holiday, and so on), and length of stay.

Economists use the term "price discrimination" for the practice of charging two people different prices for the same product (in this case, transportation service). It is not price discrimination when the difference in ticket price is associated with a different product. For example, charging more for a first-class seat, which includes a great meal and more leg room, compared to an economy seat, would not be price discrimination. Charging different prices for the same kind of seat (either first-class or economy) would be price discrimination. It is also not price discrimination when the higher price simply covers the higher cost of delivering the product. That could be another justification of a higher fare for first-class seating. Similarly, it is not price discrimination when passengers are charged extra for frills or additional service, such as checked bags, snacks, or movies.

U.S. law makes it clear that price discrimination is not permitted. However, the particular law (the Clayton Act, enacted in 1914) makes an important exception. If the discrimination does not substantially lessen competition and does not tend to create a monopoly, then the discrimination is allowable. It appears that price discrimination in airline passenger transportation is interpreted as falling within that exception, although I am not aware that the practice has been challenged in any court of law.

Price discrimination in air transportation began in the 1960s when half-price fare for youths willing to fly standby was instituted by several airlines. The practice was later dropped and still later replaced by the detailed kind of price discrimination that we experience in our air travel today.

The airlines practice price discrimination because it enhances their profits. It is inefficient to fly an airplane with empty seats. If there are five empty seats, filling them even at $100 a passenger adds a total of $500 to revenue—even though other passengers might be paying $300 each for the flight. How much is added to cost? Additional weight is very little, so fuel costs might go up by $10. The pilot, co-pilot, and flight attendants are paid the same whether or not the seats are filled. The airline gains $490 in profit by price discrimination. The five lucky passengers gain, because they travel at low cost. Overall economic efficiency is also enhanced, because more people are being transported—and at very little additional cost.

Who loses from this type of price discrimination? Not the airline involved. Not the other passengers on the plane, except for the additional minor inconvenience of having more passengers to load and unload. The losers are the other airlines, who otherwise might have been able to charge a higher price than $100 for the flight to the same destination.

It is a matter of opinion whether this kind of price discrimination is in any way "unfair." In my view, it is not unfair to consumers, because you do not pay more just because some lucky passengers pay less and you are just as likely as the next person to get a low fare on your next trip.

Q I can trust my tangible assets, but why should I trust an abstract notion called "The Market"?

A Believe this: No matter what you think, your very behavior proves that you trust the market as much as you trust your tangible assets!

Suppose you want a loaf of bread. In principle, you could grow the wheat, thrash it, grind it, mill it, bake it, slice it, package it, and store it. Even today, it is possible to get your bread by that long and involved process—and, at some point in the past, bread was always obtained that way. But think of the tremendous effort, expense, and inconvenience of producing your own bread from start to finish. Fortunately, you don't need to do that. All you have to do is go to your local bakery or supermarket and buy the bread. Isn't it amazing that the bread is always there for you to buy?

To continue, suppose you want to buy gasoline for your car, or purchase the car itself, or a house or rental apartment, or a cell phone. You don't need to produce these items yourself; you can purchase them.

What gives you the confidence that these items are always there for your purchase? Answer: The market. You trust that there are marketplaces where you can transact in goods and services—in your case and as a consumer, where you can buy these commodities. And you better have such trust. Otherwise, as a rational person, you should include in your "survival skills" how to produce on your own any good or service that you want to consume. The consequence would be that you would produce very little variety of goods and services and that your standard of living would fall tremendously.

Somehow firms together are producing enough of each commodity that consumers want to purchase. Why do they do this? They do it because it enables them to make profits. It is the self-interest of firms (or, rather, the self-interest of the firms' owners) that induces them to bring to market the commodities that consumers want *and* are able and willing to pay for, which is the meaning of the term "consumer demand." The amazing thing is that *the firms care only about their own profits and not about the welfare of consumers or the efficiency of the economy.* Nevertheless, as a result of the firms' actions, consumer demand is satisfied and the overall economy benefits! Private, self-interested behavior brings about social gain.

How does that happen? The market price acts as a signal to producers and consumers. If consumer demand for a commodity increases (perhaps because the health benefits of bread are advertised, for example), then the market price goes up. Seeing the higher price, producers (that is, the firms) produce more of the commodity, because that enhances their profits. Firms not previously producing the commodity begin to do so—to get at the profits. And these actions of firms lower the price from its higher level, possibly even to the original price. Consumers get more of the commodity for which their demand increases, and possibly at the very same price as before.

Following the terminology of Adam Smith, who wrote in the year 1776, the firms are "led by an invisible hand" to do good for consumers and bring about efficiency for the overall economy—even though the firms have no intention whatsoever of doing so. All that they care about are their profits. Yet, in doing well for themselves, the firms also do good for society. Yes, under free-market competition, firms typically "do good (for society) and do well (for themselves)" at the same time!

A similar process happens via consumer behavior. If (perhaps because of improved technology) it becomes cheaper to produce a commodity, the market price falls. Therefore consumers have an incentive to buy more of the commodity. Even though consumers are interested only in their own welfare, they increase their purchases, which are the firms' sales, of the now-cheaper commodity. And that helps the producers of the commodity and also enhances economic efficiency.

The "invisible hand" means that the self-interest of producers benefits consumers as well, and the self-interest of consumers benefits producers as well. Further, in both cases, there is improved operation of the overall economy. For the invisible hand to work, the market must provide the correct prices. Usually, the market displays correct prices, and that is why you can trust—and indeed do trust—the market.

Why do price increases sometimes increase demand rather than reduce it?

That could happen if the purchasers of the commodity expect the price increases to be followed by further price increases. For example, higher prices of stocks could give rise to the expectation of further increases. As the demand for stocks goes up, so do stock prices. This is an example of "self-justifying expectations," and the same process could apply to an increase in the price of a commodity or of commodities in general. If consumers observe inflation, they could expect further inflation. They buy consumer goods at the higher price, because they expect that prices will go up even more. The higher demand itself pushes up the prices.

At other times, it just *appears* as if price increases bring about greater demand, when in fact the reverse is true. Suppose consumers decide to buy more chocolate, because scientific research finds health benefits for the commodity. Then, the price of chocolate goes up; but the increased demand for chocolate is due to the health benefits, which increased the demand and thus the price, not due to the price increases themselves.

The idea that a higher price in and of itself increases demand is theoretically possible but extremely unlikely. In fact, economists are so confident that a higher price, in and of itself, *reduces* demand that they call that theory the "law of demand."

What is the "consumer price index"?

The "consumer price index" (CPI) measures the change in the cost of a "basket" of goods and services purchased by a typical consumer.

Chapter 5

GOVERNMENT AND THE ECONOMY (HELP OR HINDRANCE)

Economists have a love–hate relationship with government policy that affects the economy—and almost all government policy falls into that category. On the one hand, government is needed to provide good things, such as national defense, police and fire protection, and a legal system, as well as to enact and enforce laws to curb pollution and other bad things. On the other hand, governments raise taxes to finance these functions, and taxes have inefficiencies even when they do good. Also, governments often undertake policies for the advantage of specific people or specific firms, rather than for the overall benefit of society. Further, even when its objective is good, government can do bad. In this chapter, *Everyday Economics* looks at government activity with a skeptical eye.

Q Why do some states have sales taxes and others do not?

A Actually, almost all states have a sales tax. At last count, only four states (Alaska, Delaware, New Hampshire, and Oregon) do not. Some states rely more heavily on an income tax or a gross-receipts business tax for their revenue. Seven states have no income tax, and two more tax only interest-and-dividend income. Eight states have a gross-receipts tax. States must obtain revenue from some source, and usually more than one source is utilized. There is only one state without any of these three taxes, and that is Alaska. That lucky state obtains the bulk of its revenue from taxes on oil and natural-gas production. Alaska has a gasoline tax, but the tax rate per gallon is the lowest among the 50 states. Alaska does have excise taxes on alcohol and cigarettes.

The sales tax is levied at the retail level, while the gross-receipts tax is at the company level. Both taxes assess a percentage of the tax base, which is the dollar value of consumer purchases or the dollar value of business revenue. Both are regressive taxes; that is, lower-income people pay a higher percentage of their income toward the tax than do higher-income people. The reason is that lower-income people save a smaller percentage of their income than do higher-income people, and thus they spend a higher percentage of their income on consumer goods and services. In that respect, the sales tax is generally considered to be "unfair."

The income tax is usually set up to be progressive—higher tax rates for higher income brackets. So higher-income individuals pay more as a percentage of income. Rarely is the income tax a "flat tax," the same tax rate for all income levels. That tax structure is also deemed "unfair," because the rich pay the same percentage of their income as do the poor.

A problem with any tax assessed at the state level is varying tax rates. States with high income taxes (meaning tax rates) can lose inhabitants (and, to some extent, businesses) to states with lower income taxes. States with gross-receipts taxes can lose businesses to states with no gross-receipts taxes. States with a high sales tax rate can have their local businesses lose sales to businesses in states with a low (even zero) sales tax rate. Because some firms make their location decisions based on all taxes, it is possible that a state with a high sales tax rate can compensate via low income tax rates.

However, when it comes to avoidance of the sales tax, the existence of other types of tax is irrelevant. Consumers can travel to a neighboring state with a lower sales tax and purchase commodities there. Clever people can "arbitrage," meaning that they achieve a sure profit by buying goods in low sales-tax states and selling them in high sales-tax states. There are problems of transportation and transactions costs, as well as legal issues. But the incentive to avoid sales taxes of high sales-tax states is certainly there.

Of the three taxes, the sales tax is the most susceptible to tax avoidance, because it is easier, cheaper, and more convenient to ship commodities across state lines than for households or businesses to migrate across state lines. The implication is that it would be wise for states to harmonize their sales tax rates, meaning have them at the same, or nearly the same, level.

Any tax is economically inefficient, because it makes people and firms do what they would not want to do if there were no tax. Two characteristics of the sales tax make it preferable to excise taxes, which are per-unit taxes levied on particular commodities. First, the sales tax is uniform across all commodities, although there can be exemptions (services, medical supplies, food) that vary with each state. Except for exemptions, a uniform tax affects all commodities equally. That means less inefficiency, because no particular commodity is hit with an exceptionally high tax and therefore exceptional cutback of sales at the resulting high price.

Second, the sales tax is assessed as a percentage of the dollar value of purchases or sales (purchases are from the standpoint of the consumer and sales from the standpoint of the retailer; the amount is the same). This means that the tax, and hence inflation-adjusted tax revenue, is not diminished by inflation. In contrast, a tax per unit of a commodity (per gallon of gasoline or per pack of cigarettes, for example) converts to a smaller percentage tax as inflation proceeds. For instance, a $1 tax per gallon of gasoline is equivalent to a 50 percent percentage tax when the price of gasoline is $2 per gallon but only a 25 percent tax when the price is $4. That advantage of the sales tax is important for tax revenue, since the state budget could go into deficit if expenditures rise with inflation (as they naturally do) while revenues do not.

Q Why do states tax alcohol and tobacco so heavily? Is it because they are "sin taxes"?

A You are no doubt right that alcohol and tobacco are good candidates for an excise tax, at least in part because they are viewed as commodities that are "sinful." An excise tax is a tax per unit sold: per pack of cigarettes or per unit-volume of alcohol. (Of course, it is illegal to sell either alcohol or tobacco to minors.)

One reason to tax alcohol and tobacco is that it is politically safe, even popular, to hit these commodities with high taxes. The ultimate reason for this is that alcohol and tobacco are unpopular commodities, at least to those who do not consume them. That is not the only reason these products are so highly taxed. High taxes raise retail prices and therefore discourage purchases and consumption. This is especially true for individuals with low income, presumably young people. If it is a social goal to reduce alcohol drinking and cigarette smoking, especially by young people, then high taxes attempt to accomplish that goal.

Another purpose in taxing alcohol and tobacco is to raise revenue. These products are good candidates for that purpose, because they have addictive properties. Nicotine is addictive to virtually everyone, and alcohol is addictive to some people. If addiction is involved, then the increase in price from taxation cuts purchases only slightly. So cigarette tax revenue, which is the product of the per-unit tax (tax per pack of cigarettes) and the number of units (packs of cigarettes) sold, usually increases when the tax goes up. A much higher per-unit tax multiplying an only slightly lower number of packs sold results in higher revenue. A similar argument applies to alcohol, although probably the cutback in purchases would be more substantial.

For more revenue from an excise tax, the government does not want purchases to be cut back. In other words, the two purposes of taxing alcohol and tobacco—to reduce consumption and increase revenue—are contradictory.

It is arguable that low-income individuals take care of their health less than high-income individuals do, perhaps because they have less medical care or less access to health-care information. So low-income individuals would be more inclined to drink alcohol to excess and smoke cigarettes. It is also arguable that poorer people have fewer recreational alternatives than richer people, and therefore may be more likely to buy alcohol or tobacco in lieu of purchasing tickets to plays, musical performances, and athletic events. Therefore the excise taxes on alcohol and cigarettes are "regressive," meaning that they take a higher percentage of the income of low-income individuals than of high-income individuals. That kind of tax—as a percent of income, hitting poor people harder than rich people—is generally considered to be unfair.

New York City has rent control. Is that a good policy?

Absolutely not. Rent control is an example of government good intention leading to a bad outcome. It is amazing that rent control still exists in New York City, even after having been abandoned by many other municipalities. Rent control is intended to help poor people who are tenants. But what happens is the opposite.

Look first at the demand side: people who live, or want to live, in apartments. Apart from a group of tenants lucky enough to have rent-controlled apartment units in well-managed buildings, almost everyone suffers. With rent control, the price of some apartment units is below the free-market price. So a lot more people want apartments, and there is a scarcity of available apartments. Who gets the apartments? Those who are lucky, or who already are in the apartments, or who have "connections" (political or real estate), or who are willing to break the law (make side payments to the landlords or landladies). Further, those already in rent-controlled units are reluctant to move, for that would mean having to pay market rent. But if their family situation changes, they may want to move—except that it would not be in their financial best interest to do so. That is frustrating both to those stuck in rent-controlled units turned undesirable for them and to those who want to move into these apartments.

Worse is what happens on the supply side: the behavior of the apartment-building owners. If the allowable rent is so low that it does not permit the building owner to make a profit, the building will not be maintained, necessary repairs will be ignored, and—worst-case scenario—the building could be abandoned, with back taxes piling up and dire effects on the neighborhood.

But one group of tenants does gain from rent control: tenants and prospective tenants of luxury units. Rent control does not apply to luxury apartments. So virtually all new residential construction in New York City is either for luxury apartments or condominiums (obviously not affected by rent control), or for public housing (for which rent control is irrelevant). With more luxury apartment buildings, the rent on luxury units is lower than otherwise.

Bottom line: Rent control, which is established to help poor and middle-class tenants, ends up helping politically connected and wealthy tenants.

How do subsidies work?

Subsidies are the opposite of taxes. The government *gives* money to individuals or firms, instead of *collecting* money from individuals or firms. Subsidies can take several forms. A firm could be given a fixed dollar amount if it behaves in a certain way; for example, switching from a polluting to a nonpolluting production process. Similarly, an individual could be given welfare payments (which is a form of subsidy) if he takes a job-retraining program. (Of course, it is possible to have welfare without a retraining program.)

A subsidy can be a fixed total dollar amount, called a "lump-sum subsidy," because the recipient gets a lump-sum payment that cannot be increased no matter what he does. A bank could be given $2 billion dollars to use as it sees fit. A poor family could be provided $10,000 annually to spend as it wishes. Or, the subsidy can be a fixed number of dollars *per unit of activity*—called a "per-unit subsidy." Auto companies could be given a subsidy of $1,000 for each electric or hybrid car that they produce. A school system could receive $100 from the state for each student registered on the first day of school. A household could get $100 monthly from the government for each natural or adopted minor child. As the examples show, subsidies can go to businesses as much as to individuals. In fact, "bailouts" to business often take the form of subsidies.

Subsidies have two different purposes. First, the objective could be to keep the recipient going, whether the recipient is an individual or a firm. Without the subsidy (welfare payment), the individual— or dependents under his care—might be unable to pay the rent or get enough food. Without the subsidy, the bailed-out firm might go bankrupt, thus ceasing to exist as an independent entity.

The second possible objective of a subsidy is to change behavior. The government wants children to be educated, so it provides an incentive for the school system to get the children in the school from day one. The government wants more energy-efficient cars on the road, so it gives auto manufacturers a dollar amount for each electric or hybrid car produced. Note that the per-unit subsidy means that, for each unit (in this case, electric or hybrid car) produced, the cost of making the unit is reduced. Therefore the firm gets a larger profit, revenue minus cost, for each unit produced. The firm can increase its overall profit by increasing production—and, normally, that is what it does. The subsidy works!

Are subsidies good or bad? Obviously, they are good for whoever receives them. They might have some social value or accomplish some economic efficiency. But subsidies have to be paid for. So taxpayers in general pay for subsidies that particular individuals and firms receive. Suppose the government borrows the funds for the subsidies. It doesn't matter—again taxpayers are hit with interest payments on the loans (or bonds issued) and must also repay the principal.

An argument can be made that just a little money is taken from a lot of people and businesses—and then a lot of money is made available to give to just a few people and a few businesses (meaning a few in comparison to the number of people and businesses taxed). After all, the small amount of money taken away would hardly make any difference in the lives of those taxed, while the large amount of money that each gets would make a big difference to the recipients of the subsidy.

That is a good argument, but it does carry with it the implication that *the number of recipients of subsidies should be small.* If everyone is given a subsidy, any good effects vanish. If everyone is given a lot of welfare payments, there would be hardly any work, and therefore a lot less output, in the economy. If every business firm is given a per-unit subsidy to increase output, the wages of labor and prices of materials would go up, and the subsidy would not be effective. There is only so much labor and raw materials and buildings and land to go around.

What is a bailout? Why are bailouts always for large companies rather than for small businesses? And are bailouts a good idea in the first place?

A "bailout" is a rescue of a company from going bankrupt due to financial difficulties. The company cannot pay its debts or fulfill its contractual obligations. In legal terms, the firm is, or is about to be, "insolvent," meaning unable to make good on its debts. The government steps in with aid to keep the company operating.

The most common bailout policies are the government making a loan to the firm, guaranteeing loans that banks make to the firm, or even providing the firm with funds that do not have to be paid back. Sometimes it is felt that the company cannot possibly survive—even with any such aid. In that case, the government may instead make loans to another firm, with the stipulation that this firm will take over the financially strapped firm. The faltering firm is usually either a bank or another financial institution, or a manufacturing company.

Some bailout policies are tailor-made for banks and similar financial institutions. A controversial policy is the government buying "bad loans" or "bad (sour) securities" from banks in difficulty. If the government pays a market price for the loans or securities—meaning a price that the loans or securities would sell for in the marketplace—then it is a mild kind of bailout. But if the government offers a price above what the loans or securities would command in the market, then the bailout is serious. Another policy is guaranteeing deposits of customers of the bank, or of increasing the money limits of existing guarantees.

There are three reasons why a bailout could be a good idea. One situation is to keep a company going when it is only temporarily in financial straits. For example, if it had time to recover when consumer demand for its product increased, the company could survive and pay back any government loan. A second situation is when a company is "too big to fail." This is why only big companies get bailouts. When could the company be "too big to fail"? It could employ a lot of workers or be a crucial supplier to other large companies, or it could be a bank so connected with other banks via borrowing and lending that the bank failing could have a devastating effect on the banking system—or so the government or central bank believes. A third situation is when there is widespread fear of insolvency throughout the financial system. In that case the entire financial sector could be the recipient of a bailout—for example, by the government or central bank buying up bad securities owned by banks.

There are important arguments against a bailout. If it is expected that similar bailouts will continue to take place, then in the future firms may take risks contrary to sound business practice. They would do so, secure in the knowledge that if their risky decisions turn out badly, the government would bail them out. The incentive that bailouts give to unsound risk-taking behavior is called "moral hazard."

Another argument, just as important, is the fact that a bailout keeps inefficient, poorly managed firms in operation. This means that efficient, well-managed firms do not enter the industry or, if already in the industry, do not expand as much as if the weak firms were allowed to fail. The result is that productivity in the industry is lower and prices to consumers are higher. That undesirable outcome would not happen if insolvent firms were allowed to fail. If the firms cannot continue to operate in the market on their own, then in a bailout the government is assuming that it knows more than the market (in effect, the government is saying "the market is wrong in letting the firms fail").

Finally, any bailout must be financed—and guess who pays? You're right; it's the taxpayer. To many people, it does not seem fair that general tax revenue is used to bail out specific companies that are probably in trouble through their own bad business decisions.

How does a corporation actually go bankrupt?

In the United States, bankruptcy law provides two fundamentally different ways in which corporations can go bankrupt: liquidation and reorganization. Liquidation happens under Chapter 7 of bankruptcy law; reorganization takes place under Chapter 11.

Under Chapter 7, the corporation ceases to exist. All of its assets are sold and the proceeds are distributed strictly according to law. The most important rule is that creditors (holders of bonds issued by the firm, banks that made loans to the firm, and suppliers of materials to the firm) must be paid off *fully* before the owners of the corporation receive any return from their equity. Also, each "class" of creditor (bondholder, supplier, and so on) is reimbursed fully (in order specified by law) before the next class gets any funds whatsoever. The only bright side for the owners of the firm—the stockholders—is that they have no legal liability except for their investment in the equity of the firm. So, unlike an individual filing for bankruptcy, stockholders retain their other financial holdings and all their physical possessions. Also, their present and future income cannot be seized to pay off the corporation's debts.

Under Chapter 11, the corporation continues to do business, usually under its current management. Creditors are paid off from the firm's future earnings, not from selling the firm's assets. The rules for reimbursing the creditors are different from those of Chapter 7. Most creditors have their claims satisfied only in part, and even the stock-holders can get some return on their equity. A problem with Chapter 11 is that, for the reorganization to take place, there must be agreement among classes of creditors, although within each class unanimity is not required. This involves a negotiation process that takes time; sometimes a long time. During this period, the firm can see its revenue dwindle and its losses mount. Reason: The firm loses both customers and employees, and the firms' suppliers insist on tougher terms. All these parties fear either that negotiations may fail and the firm may instead be liquidated (Chapter 7 bankruptcy) or that the firm may enter Chapter 11 but ultimately fail anyway (again, Chapter 7).

Why a firm goes bankrupt is an interesting question. Sometimes the firm has lost competitive standing in its industry. The firm's technology is obsolete, or its workers are paid more than in other firms. Sometimes the industry itself has become obsolete—think typewriters versus word processors, and word processors versus personal computers—and the firm's competitiveness within its industry is irrelevant.

Sometimes management has made decisions that are in its own interest but not in the interest of the owners. For example, managers may want corporate jets and large staffs, or are interested only in current profits and not in long-run profits. The divorce of ownership (stockholders) from control (management) is one of the characteristics of the corporation that can lead to poor decision making from the standpoint of the owners. Sometimes managers engage in illegal activity, such as taking money from the firm's coffers—money that rightfully belongs to the stockholders.

Q Why is there a food shortage around the world, when U.S. farmers are paid not to produce crops and as a nation we regularly throw out food?

A One of the great achievements of economic growth has been the improvement in agricultural productivity. The percent of the population engaged in agriculture has fallen tremendously over time, while agricultural output has also increased substantially. Certainly, that is true for industrial countries (the major developed countries, including and perhaps especially the United States). It is also increasingly true for developing countries.

Governments do not leave agricultural markets alone; they refuse to rely on the free market. But the way governments intervene differs in developed and developing countries. In the United States and other industrial countries, agriculture is heavily subsidized. Typically, the method is to have a price floor (the lowest allowable price) for a given product, combined with subsidies to farmers to ensure that their revenue is consistent with that price floor even if the market (world) price is below it. A high price floor (above the market price) has two important implications. First, urban areas are subsidizing rural areas—or nonagriculture is subsidizing agriculture. It is true that taxpayers in general are paying for the subsidy, but only agriculture gets the subsidy. In extreme terms, poor urban people are guaranteeing the income of rich farmers (agribusiness). If that doesn't seem fair, it's because it is not fair by any reasonable definition of fairness. It is also true that interfering with the free market in agriculture reduces economic efficiency. Inefficient farms have an incentive to remain in business, to collect the subsidies.

Second, farmers have an incentive to overproduce, meaning to produce more than they would if there were no price floor (or rather, if the price floor were not above the free-market price for the product). There is overproduction: At the high price, consumers buy less of the product than they would at the lower, free-market price.

So, the government established the price floor, and farmers are producing more than they can sell. To make good on their pro-agricultural policy, the government buys up the excess production. Now the "price floor" becomes more than that; it becomes a "price support." What does the government do with all the agricultural products that are piling up? The food can be given to the domestic poor or to school-lunch programs. The food can also be given away as foreign aid to poor, developing countries, but this type of foreign aid has been criticized as detrimental to agriculture in the recipient countries. Their farmers cannot compete with the artificially low price associated with U.S. foreign aid in the form of actual food. The food typically is sold to consumers at a price to cover transportation and transactions cost.

To avoid piling up so many agricultural surplus products, the government sometimes does pay farmers not to produce certain crops; you are quite right. If that seems to be a stupid policy, it follows from the prior policy of the guaranteed support for the floor price. It could be cheaper to pay farmers to produce less than to buy up the surplus.

Agricultural policy in developing countries is typically quite different. Far from being subsidized, agriculture is taxed and/or hit with low price ceilings. The purpose is to benefit city dwellers, both via government spending of the tax proceeds in urban areas and via cheap food. However, farmers have incentive to produce less crops, not more—exactly the opposite incentive in the United States and other developed countries. (There is a movement to change this policy in some, but far from all, developing countries.)

So the basic reason for a food shortage in developing countries is the policy of squeezing agriculture in favor of industry, of taxing rural areas for the benefit of urban areas—the opposite of what happens in industrial countries. The developing country's government thinks that industrial development is thereby fostered, but that does not happen to any measurable extent. Instead, industrial workers and consumers in general suffer because of recurrent food shortages. In fact, laws keeping food prices down tend to be disobeyed in urban areas, and food prices actually rise above what they would be in a free market.

As far as Americans wasting food, that happens because we are a rich country. Having sufficient income for our basic needs, we are willing to waste food if it saves time or effort. However, our agricultural sector is extremely efficient and typically does not waste food or the ingredients in food production. Any waste of consequence in the United States is at the consumer level rather than at the producer level. In contrast, in developing countries, inefficiencies in transportation and laws that assign food output to specific regions can result in substantial waste of food even before the food reaches the urban consumer.

It would make a lot of good economic sense in terms of efficiency if developed countries like the United States abandoned their agricultural price supports and developing countries ended their exploitation of their agricultural sector.

Q What is the economic impact of the worsening environment? What are the economic implications of turning it around?

A Pollution is what economists call a "negative externality" or "detrimental externality." The pollution is typically generated by a business firm as part of its productive activity, but the culprit could be individuals or government. Pollution is an *externality,* because other entities (individuals, businesses) are *incidentally* affected by the pollution. It is not the *intention* of the polluting firm; the pollution happens as a by-product of the firm's normal economic activity. Pollution is a negative or detrimental activity, because it has bad consequences for those incidentally affected.

Economically, the pollution reduces costs, and therefore enhances profits, of the polluting firm. The firm has use of the clean air, the clean water, the clean soil—and uses up some of the cleanliness, without charge. If the firm had to pay for cleaning up the environmental damage or for pollution-abatement equipment that would prevent the pollution in the first place, the firm's costs would go up and its profits down. It is conceivable that the firm could not even survive economically if it did not have free use of the environment; it could go bankrupt.

The contamination of the environment hurts other firms (for example, agriculture or fishing) and it also harms individuals (by reducing the quality of life and endangering health, via contaminated air, water, or land). Some environmental damage, such as "greenhouse gas emissions," has serious implications for climate change. The long-term economic effects are uncertain but possibly profound.

The economic implications of turning pollution around would be less production of commodities associated with pollution, more production of pollution-abatement equipment, and more production of commodities that do not involve pollution. That would mean a higher quality of life for inhabitants of the country and indeed the world.

How to turn it around? One policy is direct control of emissions. For example, automobiles are required to have a catalytic converter to reduce pollution associated with the internal combustion engine. Another policy is the encouragement of new, "green" (environmentally friendly) products. For example, an electric car would not directly pollute the environment, although the electricity for the car would have to be produced in some way that might involve environmental damage (such as the construction of dams for hydroelectric power).

Taxing firms for their emissions of pollution or taxing the activity that involves the emissions is another method. A further technique is the issuance, sometimes via auction, of tradable emissions permits ("licenses to pollute"). These are more efficient ways of controlling pollution. You don't want zero pollution, because it would take up a tremendous amount of the country's workforce and capital to clean up all the pollution. There wouldn't be enough workers and capital left to produce the other things that we want. In fact, it is impossible to achieve the goal of zero pollution, because, as pollution is reduced under any policy, it gets harder and harder to cut down on the remaining pollution.

Taxing emissions and having tradable emissions permits allow firms that can most cheaply curb pollution to do so. Other firms can satisfy the law by paying the tax or buying the permits. As indicated above, reducing pollution has a cost in terms of resources (physical capital, labor, human capital [trained and educated labor], and so on). Economic efficiency requires that, to reduce pollution by a specified amount or to bring pollution down to a certain level, the cost should be as little as possible.

So all is good, provided that the government establishes the "correct" amount of tax or the "correct" amount of emissions allowable by permit. Economists have developed "cost–benefit analysis" to determine the correct amount, but in practice it is very hard to determine the correct amount of tax or pollution permits. The benefits of preventing or alleviating environmental damage are generally widespread, and it is not clear to what extent the benefits are largely in the future and to what extent "the future is now." Assumptions, not always realistic or defensible, must be made to determine the correct amount of tax or permit.

The situation is even more complex when international agreement is involved, as with the Kyoto Protocol, the purpose of which is to reduce emissions of greenhouse gases and therefore "save the atmospheric environment." Each country wants a better environment, but each country prefers that other countries curb their own greenhouse gas emissions to achieve it. Reason: Countries want to retain their economic production without the cost of pollution abatement. So it is not surprising that developing countries insist that they be excused from actively participating in the emissions reduction and that certain developed countries (including the United States) resist their own participation.

Q Can poverty ever go away?

A That depends on how poverty is defined. The United States has an official poverty line, also called a "poverty threshold." The poverty line was originally computed in the years 1963 to 1964 as three times the cost of food under an "economy food plan." Each year since then, that original poverty line has been updated using the consumer price index to adjust for inflation. For a specific year, the poverty line increases with family size, and decreases if the head of household (called "householder") is 65 years and over. Therefore "poverty lines" is the more accurate term, even for a given year, but the singular "poverty line" is conventionally used.

Then, in principle, each U.S. family has its income compared with the poverty line specific to the family's size and composition; that is, the number of related children under age 18, and whether the householder is age 65 and over. In practice, a sample of families is taken. If the family income falls below the poverty line, then each member of the family is officially determined to be "in poverty." Obviously, it is possible for each and every family to be above the poverty line. The reason is that the poverty line is an "absolute concept," constructed without reference to the distribution of family incomes during the year in question. So, yes, official U.S. poverty can go away.

There is controversy about the computation of family income when it is compared with the poverty line. Only *money* income is included, both earned income and welfare payments. Non-cash benefits (such as food stamps and housing subsidies) are not counted. That could be of importance to many families who are officially in poverty.

There is another way of calculating the number of people in poverty, though it has never been adopted in the United States. A family could be considered to be in poverty if its income is below a certain percentage of median income. Median income is the income level at which 50 percent of families fall on or above *and* at which 50 percent of families fall on or below. Let's say that the government selects the percentage as 75. So your family income has to be at least at 75 percent median family income; otherwise your family is considered in poverty. Now it can be very difficult to eliminate poverty, because it would involve making family incomes substantially more equal.

Yet a third way of computing poverty is subjective. Each householder could be asked his opinion of what level of income is just sufficient to keep his family out of poverty. In other words, the poverty line would be determined by families themselves. Under this system, which also has never been used to generate official U.S. poverty numbers, it would be almost impossible to eliminate poverty. Why? Because people would tend to adjust their own "poverty level" to fit their circumstances. Suppose people wanted to be officially in poverty, so that they would be eligible for welfare payments. Looking for a job? The self-defined poverty level is likely to be high enough so that your current income is below that level. Having trouble making mortgage payments? Again, one would state a high poverty line in order to maintain eligibility for welfare. These examples reflect self-interest determining behavior, which is a good part of economics.

No matter how poverty is defined, reducing poverty is an established objective of government. One way to reduce—and in principle even eliminate—poverty is to subsidize families in poverty sufficient to get them over the poverty line. Note that the official U.S. measurement of family income that is used to compare with the applicable poverty line already includes welfare payments and, in general, all cash subsidies to people. The number of people in poverty remains substantial; therefore, the existing policy has been too weak to be effective in removing all families from poverty.

Another suggested policy is to have strict antidiscrimination laws to protect minorities. Official U.S. poverty figures show that the percentage of African American and Latino families in poverty—meaning below the poverty line—is consistently and substantially greater than the number of other groups (non-Latino whites and Asian Americans). To the extent that this result is due to discrimination against African Americans and Latinos, stronger anti-discrimination laws could be helpful.

Many economists believe that the ultimate cause of poverty—even for minorities, at least in the twenty-first century—is a lack of "human capital," meaning inadequate education, training, and work experience. The proof of this statement is that well-educated or well-trained minorities, especially in the professions and in the military, have income levels just about the same as equally educated or equally trained non-Latino whites. Educational experts tend to agree that, if education is the key for the effective fighting of poverty, education must begin when the child is very young—preferably in preschool.

Other social observers consider the poverty problem to stem ultimately from family structure. They note that single-female householders of all races have high poverty rates. Their solution is to reestablish the two-parent family universally and to have both parents involved in the raising, especially the education, of children. Critics of this view point out that, even though a family may have a single-female householder, other relatives can substitute for an absent father. These relatives include grandparents, aunts, uncles, and older siblings.

Another diagnosis is that poverty is in large part due to labor-market rigidities, such as the minimum wage and unions. The minimum wage leads to unemployment of the least-productive, least-experienced workers. That means high-school dropouts. The minimum wage also gives scope for businesses to practice discrimination against racial minorities, because there are less people to be hired and more people looking for jobs (people like high-school dropouts are pulled in because of the high minimum wage). Unions can have rules (or agreements with firms) that make it difficult for new workers to be hired unless they join the union and are paid the high union wage. So unions tend to reduce job availability. It follows that eliminating the minimum wage and a continuing trend of fewer and fewer workers in private-sector unions could be useful in reducing poverty levels.

Finally, there are economists who see a booming economy as the best weapon to fight poverty *and* discrimination. When the economy is expanding, businesses need to hire more workers—and playing a discrimination game becomes self-evidently detrimental to profits. Even inexperienced workers tend to be hired, because it becomes the logical thing to do when experienced workers become scarce. It follows that avoiding downturns in the economy, or at least trying to have economic expansions that last much longer than recessions, is an effective anti-poverty and anti-discrimination policy. Unfortunately, that is not always easy to do.

In sum, it is theoretically possible for poverty to be eliminated—but very, very unlikely. However, poverty can be alleviated and even reduced by government policy and by a lot of luck in the form of a steadily growing economy that avoids recessions.

Q How do other countries pay for their universal health care—would that work for the United States?

A The United States is unique among high-income developed countries in lacking universal health care. There are government programs, such as Medicare and Medicaid, that provide insurance (some free, some at subsidized rates) to all individuals in a certain group (such as the elderly or qualified poor). There is some direct government delivery of medical care (primarily for veterans). There is also legislation requiring hospitals to render emergency care to all. But there is no universally guaranteed medical care.

Other countries finance their universal care in a variety of ways: taxation, compulsory public insurance, compulsory private insurance, optional private "add-on" insurance, and direct public provision of care. Often a combination of these techniques is used. The experience of other developed countries suggests that universal health care could "work" for the United States under a variety of funding methods.

There are some basic issues in shifting from the U.S. nonuniversal health care to a universal system. One problem is a possible trade-off of quality for quantity. More people will be covered under universal care, but would the quality of care be adversely affected? Simple logic states that, with an increased demand for medical care and a fixed supply of medical care, there is less care available per person. The result is that the quality of care or the timeliness of care is adversely affected. In public debate, the question is often put as follows: "Would extending insurance coverage to the one-third of Americans lacking assured health care ruin the quality of care for the two-thirds of Americans already enjoying medical insurance or direct access to medical care?"

There are two obvious solutions to this dilemma. The supply of medical care—doctors, nurses, clinics, hospitals, and so on—could increase. The per-capita demand for medical care could decrease. The latter could happen by prohibition of "unnecessary" medical care. The increase in supply would involve a decrease in supply of other goods and services in the economy. The decrease in demand could have a profound affect on the psyche of currently insured Americans.

Take orthopedic services in the United States as an example. Good insurance means that you can readily receive an MRI within 24 hours. Short of an emergency, service that fast is virtually impossible in Canada. In fact, Canada sometimes satisfies its "excess demand" (demand beyond available supply) for medical care by shipping patients to the United States for treatment! How will that work if and when the

United States itself adopts universal health care, with consequent enhanced demand for health services?

Another issue is how to finance universal health care. Yes, that is the point of your question; but the amount of health care is likely to be even greater than it is now. It is unlikely that Americans with current health insurance will tolerate a reduction in their care, even if they are pleased with seeing health care extended to the rest of the population. So the cost of financing the universal health-care system is likely to be greater than financing health care with the present nonuniversal system. The issue of a possible change in the method of financing merges with the issue of an increase in the total amount of financing.

The only way for universal health care to be established in the United States is by a political consensus. If the program is financed by taxation, and especially higher rates of taxation on high-income brackets or on businesses, then economic efficiency and consequently total output (GDP, gross domestic product) could deteriorate. It is possible that the extension of health care to all residents of the country would carry with it a reduced ability to finance the current amount of health care *per person covered.* It could still be a rational policy to adopt universal health care, but it behooves politicians and the government to be aware of the financial and general economic consequences.

On the plus side, universal health care could reduce emergency medical situations and generally improve the health of individuals currently without adequate or any medical insurance. Over time, that could act to reduce the amount of financing health care. Also, the quality and hence the productivity of the workforce would be improved.

Q What are the arguments for incentives versus disincentives?

A You can get a person (or a business) to change behavior either by the promise of a reward if he carries out the stipulated change in behavior or by the threat of a punishment if he does not carry out the stipulated change in behavior. The promise of reward is called an incentive, or a positive incentive; the threat of punishment is a disincentive, or negative incentive.

Examples abound. To induce firms to reduce pollution, the government could subsidize them if they do so; tax them if they do not. To get people to stop smoking, the government could tax cigarettes or subsidize "stop smoking" classes. To cut down on school absenteeism, students could be hit with detention if absent or be given pizza and ice cream if in attendance. To prevent auto accidents, there are high auto-insurance premiums for drivers with a history of causing accidents; low premiums for drivers without such a history. (That example involves symmetrical positive and negative incentives.) To increase domestic production of a commodity, the government could impose a tariff on imports of the commodity or provide a subsidy to domestic production.

There is a certain commonsense logic that the direct policy, whether incentive or disincentive, is preferred. If the objective is to *reduce* the amount of something (smoking, pollution, absenteeism, etc.), then a disincentive makes more sense. If the objective is to *increase* the amount of something, then an incentive is called for. Don't pay people to stop smoking; punish them if they continue to smoke. Don't tax people if they don't wear their seat belt; reward them if they do.

But that argument is simplistic. Reducing the amount of something is often another way of increasing the amount of something else, and vice versa. To reduce absenteeism is to increase attendance. To reduce pollution is to increase clean air. So the direct-versus-indirect argument is not a productive way of deciding on incentive or disincentive.

In principle, in each case, either an incentive or a disincentive could accomplish the same objective, providing the incentive and disincentive are each calibrated appropriately. One problem is that the calibration—the amount of the incentive or disincentive—need not be the same. It might take either less or more incentive than disincentive to get the same result. Reason: In any given situation, people and businesses could have a greater or a lesser response to an incentive than a disincentive. There could be a measurement problem here; the incentive and disincentive might not be comparable. Even so, they might be able to be compared in terms of monetary cost. For example, to reduce school absenteeism by 20 students each day, it might cost $100 to pay a school staff member to supervise detention (punishment for absenteeism) or $8 per student for 500 students for pizza and ice cream (reward for attendance). In this example, the disincentive—detention policy—is less costly, and therefore more economically efficient.

Continuing with cost, a government subsidy has the disadvantage that it increases government expenditure, whereas a tax increases government revenue. There is another issue. In the case of pollution, there is the danger that subsidizing the reduction of pollution could induce firms to increase pollution to begin with—in order to get the subsidy for reducing pollution! Also, more firms could produce the pollution-causing commodities to get the subsidy. These unintended and perverse incentives would both increase pollution (at least prior to reduction via subsidy) and increase government spending.

Q What is "supply-side economics"? Does it really work?

A "Supply-side economics" is government policy oriented to changing the incentives of individuals and businesses concerning how much to work, how much to save, and how much to invest. For example, if the tax rate on *additional* earned income is reduced, then you might decide to work more.

Consider a teacher who has the opportunity to engage in summer teaching for additional pay. What is relevant in the decision whether to do so is the income tax rate (federal, state, and local combined) on the additional income earned via summer teaching. Even if the teacher's average tax rate (the tax rate on all income together) is only 20 percent of income, *the tax on the additional income earned (called the "marginal tax rate")* is higher, perhaps 30 percent. This means that the teacher gets to keep only 70 percent of the additional income, and may therefore decide not to teach over the summer. If the teacher could retain 80 percent or

90 percent (the marginal tax rate being 20 percent or 10 percent), the teacher might very well decide to do the extra teaching.

Of course, some people teach because they like it. They would teach summer school no matter what the tax on their additional income. But there are also some people who do respond to incentives when it comes to working more or less. Not everyone has to be concerned with incentives and disincentives—just some people—for economics to work.

The point is that any taxation of earnings or savings affects decisions to work, save, or invest—and it is always the *marginal* tax rate on additional income—not the average tax rate on all income—that is relevant. Reducing marginal tax rates should be the paramount tool of fiscal policy, according to supply-side economists. This rule is in contrast to the usual precept of fiscal policy: Reduce tax rates in general in a recession, increase taxes in general in an overheated (inflationary) economy.

Also, supply-side economists emphasize that the *highest* marginal tax rates should be reduced first and foremost, because these are the rates that affect the most-productive (as measured by highest-income or highest-earnings) individuals and businesses in the economy. This rule goes against the customary doctrine of fairness: Rich people and highly profitable businesses should pay more in taxes, because (a) they are better off, and (b) they have a greater ability to pay taxes, than poor people and less-profitable businesses.

Whether supply-side economics actually works is controversial. Some economists assert that cutting income taxes at the highest tax brackets (that is, reducing the highest marginal tax rates) has been found not only to increase the economy's output of goods and services but also to improve the government budget by increasing government revenue. The increase in work (and therefore the increase in income) is so great that people earn more income and thereby pay more taxes to the government; government tax revenue increases even though tax rates are less.

Other economists deny the beneficial supply-side effects on economic output and on government revenue. They claim that the alleged good results are due to other events in the economy. Some economists acknowledge that supply-side economics might work but reject it anyhow—on the grounds that it is unfair to reduce high tax rates (which affect the rich) instead of low tax rates (which affect the poor). As sometimes happens in economics, there is no straightforward answer.

Q What is meant by "trickle-down economics"?

A "Trickle-down economics" means that reducing taxes on business and on high-income individuals will indirectly also be of benefit to lower-income individuals and to everyone in general. People, including economists, often associate trickle-down economics with supply-side economics. But the two theories are different.

Supply-side economics says that economic efficiency and the overall economy benefit from reducing high tax rates on business and on high-income individuals—and that is all. The improvement in the overall economy may or may not benefit low-income individuals; supply-side economists do not even care. Their objective is to improve the economy as a whole.

Those who believe in trickle-down economics assert that the improvement in the overall economy will also improve the standard of living for everyone, including people with low income. The improvement would take the form of more jobs, lower prices of commodities, and better-quality products.

A quick way to understand the difference is: Supply-side policies increase the size of the economic pie, but it is not clear who gets the additional pie. Trickle-down economics asserts that some of the additional pie goes to people who were not the recipients of the reduction in taxes; that is, to low-income people.

Whether trickle-down economics works is controversial. Most economists, in their capacity as economists, do not care. The important objective is to improve the functioning of the economy: to increase the size of the economic pie, or perhaps to reduce the amount of effort (work) that it takes to keep the present size of the pie where it is. Either way, the standard of living of everyone *could* be improved.

In fact, it may not be improved for everyone. That does not sound fair, but fairness and economic efficiency are two different things. They may or may not go together. Trickle-down economics states that they do; some economists are not so sure of that.

Some observers turn trickle-down economics on its head. They claim that the opposite is true: there is "trickle-up economics." What they mean is that by *directly* improving the standard of living of the poor—by such means as job availability, health care, housing, education, and welfare in general—economic efficiency improves and economic output goes up. Then, indirectly, business profits and the standard of living even of rich people also increase.

There is some logic to trickle-up economics, but expanding the welfare system has a cost. If more economic output takes the form of universal health care, better housing for poor people, and more education, then less economic output is available for other things, such as automobiles, military spending, and video games. Trickle-up supporters would counter that this "opportunity-cost" argument, if true, applies only to the short run. Over a longer period of time, the improved health, education, and work ethic of the poorer segment of the population (beneficiaries of enhanced welfare) would improve the work availability and productivity of these people. As a consequence, the economic pie would go up substantially.

Note that trickle-down economics involves less taxes and therefore less of a role for government in the economy, whereas trickle-up economics needs higher taxes (to pay for the increased welfare) and therefore expands the government sector. The counterargument that trickle-up economics could take the form of reduced taxes for the poor (just as trickle-down economics reduces taxes on the rich) is not valid, because many low-income people (possibly already on welfare) pay little if any taxes even without trickle-up economics.

What is "voodoo economics"?

The term "voodoo economics" was first used by George H. W. Bush (the first of the Bush family to be president of the United States) in

1980, when he was campaigning for the Republican nomination for the presidency. Bush's opponent was Ronald Reagan, who eventually won the nomination. Bush invented "voodoo economics" as a derogatory term to ridicule Reagan's economic proposals. In spite of that unpleasantness, Reagan selected Bush as his vice-presidential candidate, and together they served two terms as president and vice president. In the next presidential election, Bush secured the Republican nomination, and he served as president for one term.

One interpretation of voodoo economics is that it connotes any economic policy that is inappropriate or unwise. A special case is when the policy is self-contradictory. Bush appeared to have interpreted Reagan's policy as reducing taxes and increasing government spending simultaneously, while not increasing the budget deficit. That was not a fair description of what Reagan was advocating. He was in favor of supply-side economics, which became associated with the term "Reaganomics." Supply-side economics involves reducing high marginal tax rates (meaning tax rates at the higher brackets) to encourage additional work by highly productive labor. Therefore the economy would produce more output, overall income would go up, and government tax revenue could actually increase. A somewhat different take on Reaganomics is that it did not directly affect the level of government spending: higher expenditure on the military would be compensated by lower spending on the civilian sector.

Voodoo economics now has only historical interest. The term is no longer used routinely, if at all.

How do budget deficits work? Where does the money come from and who do we owe?

Clearly, you mean the federal government budget deficit. There are various ways to compute the deficit, but basically it is government revenue from taxes and other sources *minus* government spending on goods, services, and subsidies. The deficit has to be financed, or else it could not happen. The government has to borrow the amount of the deficit. Typically, this is done by issuing bonds. The bonds are created and sold by the U.S. Treasury, and are purchased either initially or ultimately (there is a huge secondary market in government securities) by a variety of parties: financial institutions, other corporations, individuals, pension funds, individuals, foreign governments, foreign central banks, and the Federal Reserve (Fed).

When private domestic entities finance the deficit, we owe the debt to ourselves, considering the United States as a whole. Now consider the Fed buying the bonds—an open market operation. This is generally done in the secondary market. In fact, the Fed need not purchase the bonds just issued; it can buy other government bonds in the same amount as the bonds issued—the effect is the same. The Fed is essentially "printing money," thereby increasing bank reserves, with a potential multiple impact on the money stock. The effect is the same as if the Fed simply printed currency to finance the government deficit. So the Fed is really financing the deficit.

That is a combined expansionary fiscal policy and expansionary monetary policy. The fiscal policy is the government increasing direct spending on goods and services and/or reducing taxes, thus stimulating private spending on goods and services. The monetary policy is the Fed increasing bank reserves. Finally, if foreigners buy government bonds, this is an inflow of funds coming into the country; but the foreigners would have to be paid interest and repaid principal in the future.

Whether budget deficits work to expand the economy (for example, to fight a recession) is controversial. Economists offer two reasons why they might not work. First, if taxpayers look to the future, they realize that they or their descendants will eventually be assessed increased taxes to pay interest on the debt and to repay the debt. Therefore they would spend less and save more. That offsets the increased government spending. Second, financing of the deficit involves a higher demand for funds, which pushes up interest rates and reduces borrowing by individuals (to purchase items such as homes and durable goods) and businesses (to invest in physical capital). Again, the increased government spending is offset. In this case, economists say that the higher government spending "crowds out" private spending.

The budget deficit would most likely expand the economy if it is financed by the Federal Reserve. But then there may be no need for the government deficit at all. Fed open-market purchases might be all that is needed.

Even apart from fighting a recession, government deficits have another effect. Government deficits increase the size of the government sector relative to the private sector of the economy. The same is true for increased government expenditure no matter how it is financed—including entirely by taxes, in which case there is no deficit. The deficits or increased government spending mean bigger government. Note that this effect exists even if private spending is not "crowded out," but crowding out just makes it worse.

Chapter 6

FINANCIAL MARKETS (BUBBLES AND BURSTS)

Advice for your personal saving and investment was given in Chapter 3. The present chapter complements that advice by looking at the broader picture. How do financial markets and financial institutions work? The important message that *Everyday Economics* has for you here is that details of financial markets change over time—new types of institutions emerge, new types of assets are created, new ways of moving money around are developed—but the basic fact of market determination of asset prices and interest rates remains. However, that market determination does not prevent either an organization or an individual from engaging in poor investment decisions, and it decidedly does not prevent a financial institution from poor management.

What can be done to stop the next stock market crash?

Often a stock market crash is the bursting of a "bubble." A bubble is a situation in which just about everyone in the market is struck by the fact that stock prices are continually going up, which causes many people actively to buy stock, which pushes the price up even more, with the expectation that prices will continue to increase, so that more people buy stock——and on the circle goes round. Note that to participate in a bubble can be quite rational. It doesn't matter that the bubble leads to stock prices that cannot last. While the bubble goes on, there are profits to be made in the market. (Actually, the profits are a "capital gain,"—which means the excess of the price at which you sell stock over the price at which you bought the stock.) You make profits by buying stock and reselling at a higher price; others come in the market and buy, intending to resell at a still higher price (and you may buy again, as you see the price continuing to go up, confident of reselling at a still higher price)—and on the circle goes.

However, experience shows that eventually bubbles burst, and the market crashes, or goes into a downward spiral. Think of it as a reverse bubble. Now just about everyone believes that stock prices will continue to fall; therefore many market participants try to unload their stocks before prices fall too much. They actively sell their stock, which pushes stock prices down, justifying their expectation that prices will fall, which motivates still more participants actively to sell stocks—and the downward movement of prices continues.

How can the market crash, the bursting of the bubble, be prevented? You might think that one way is to keep the bubble going forever. But the stock prices would get higher and higher, until they are so far above what the "fundamentals" of the market (meaning the expected earnings of the firms whose stocks are being traded) dictate that the bubble would have to burst. So keeping the bubble going is unrealistic.

Another approach to preventing a market crash is to stop the bubble from happening in the first place. That is very difficult to do, because many investors in the stock market welcome a chance to make huge profits (capital gains). They see the market going up day after day, and want to get aboard the profit train. It is difficult to resist that temptation, not only if you are an individual investor but also if you are an institutional investor (such as a mutual fund or pension fund), because the institutional investor is under great pressure from its owners or clients to take advantage of market situations that virtually guarantee capital gains.

What if the stock exchange had a rule that prices had to have an absolute floor? The stock exchange could assign a lowest allowable price to each stock, and not allow any market transaction that was below that price. Could that prevent a crash? Not in any real sense, because investors would not want to hold stocks under these circumstances. Stocks that hit the bottom price would have continued to fall in price under a free market. Investors would try to unload the stocks, but no one would buy except at a lower price than the bottom. Frustrated investors would have stocks that have a higher nominal value than true (market) value. The stocks would then be no good, because they couldn't be sold! Even if you were amenable to selling at a lower price, that would be impossible, because the rules of the stock exchange would be violated.

In addition, corporations would have trouble issuing new stocks—and therefore raising funds for business expansion—because of suspicion that stocks could hit bottom and become essentially frozen. The stock exchange would lose its role as an intermediary between corporations that want to raise funds and investors that are prepared to provide the funds (investing in the corporations). Also, stocks would lose their ability to be sold for cash readily. No one likes to have her stocks frozen, nonsaleable and nontransferable to others. So stocks would *permanently* lose their attractiveness as an asset in which to invest. That is different from, and much more serious than, stocks *temporarily* losing their attractiveness because the market price of stocks is falling.

You might have the idea that the Federal Reserve (the Fed) or the Treasury could prevent a market crash by buying or selling stocks to keep the market on a steady path—not a bubble or boom, not a bubble burst or crash, by just keeping the market steadily moving up. But the market does not naturally behave that way. The Fed or the Treasury would be going against the market (or else why should it transact in the stock market at all?) and that carries with it several problems.

First of all, determining the "steady-path price" for each stock would involve political pressure and lobbying. A company would be favored with a high price, of course.

Second, even if that pressure and lobbying were ignored, it is not clear how a steady-path price could be computed "objectively." Does the Fed or the Treasury know any more about expected future profits of the company than the market does? Or how the expected future profits would enter the "fundamental" price of the stock? Or even whether that fundamental price should determine the steady-path price?

Third, the lending capacity of banks, and therefore the money supply, would be greatly affected by the Fed's stock market operations. As a consequence, the entire economy would also be affected—and quite possibly in ways opposite to what is desired. The Fed transacting in stocks would mess up its monetary policy. If the Treasury were to do it, it would have to obtain funds by taxation or by issuing bonds, and this would mess up its fiscal policy.

Bottom line: As long as market participants want to make a quick profit rather than be content to "buy and hold" stocks for the long haul, stock market booms and consequent crashes are inevitable. Any fix oriented to prevent stock market crashes is either effectively impossible or extremely dangerous to the overall economy.

Q How much is a stock's value based on real assets of a given company versus the perception of that company?

A If by "real assets" you mean physical plant (factories, office buildings, machinery, equipment), the answer, for many companies, is "not much." For example, Google and Microsoft have little physical capital, apart from computers and office space, but, as successful companies, their stock prices are generally high. The important assets of these companies are their brainpower, what economists call "human capital." On the other side, a firm can have a lot of physical capital—for example, automobile companies—and yet the stock price could be unusually low, because the company is not successful in selling its products.

The question is more meaningful—but unfortunately more difficult to answer—if it is rephrased: *How much is the price of a stock based on the fundamental value of the stock and how much on the perception of that fundamental value?*

Stock prices of individual companies—and composite indexes of stocks of many companies (such as the Dow Jones Industrial Average [DJIA] and Standard and Poor's [S&P] measures)—are extremely volatile. In just a few years, stock prices can double or triple during a bull market and lose half their value in a bear market. It is hard to believe that *actual* "fundamental value" can be so changeable in brief periods of time. You might want to conclude that sudden and vigorous changes in *perceptions* of fundamental value are responsible for the huge volatility. That is sometimes true. For example, it can explain how the bull market in technology stocks ignited when Silicon Valley began to roll.

However, a more common reason for stock price movement is what economists call a "bubble" and the subsequent "burst" of the bubble. (If you see an analogy to bubble gum, you are right.) A bubble is an upward movement in stock prices propelled by the belief that stock prices will continue to rise, irrespective of the fundamental value of the company or companies. In other words, the purchasers of the stock are motivated solely by speculation: They are confident that they will be able to sell the stock later at a higher price (a much higher price) than the price they paid for the stock. The belief could be well-founded, at least for a while, because virtually all market participants are thinking that way; so we do not judge that the speculators are engaged in irrational behavior.

Inevitably the stock price becomes so high relative to its fundamental value that "the bubble bursts" and stock prices go into a downward spiral. Now expectations of virtually all market participants are that the stock price will continue to go down. It is rational, at least for a while, to sell the stock. Most likely, this will take the form of contracting to sell the stock in the future when the price is expected to be lower than the contracted price; the stock can then be bought at the lower price for the contracted sale and a profit would be earned. (Normally, the stock is borrowed at the outset; so in principle the stock can be sold irrespective of the future price.) Eventually the stock price becomes so low, relative to its fundamental value, that the fall in prices stops and reverses itself.

Bubbles and bursting bubbles can occur for the stock price of one company, for the stock prices of all companies in a particular industry, and for virtually all companies in all sectors of the economy. However, not all movements of stock prices are due to bubbles and their bursts. There are periods of stability, or rather steady upward movement, in stock prices.

So how much of a stock price is based on the fundamental value of the stock, how much on perceptions of the value, and how much on bubbles and bubbles bursting? No one knows. Some financial advisors advocate "value investing": if the actual price of a stock is below its fundamental value, buy the stock; if the price is above fundamental value, sell the stock. The problem is that we don't know how to obtain the fundamental value of a stock.

That lack of knowledge doesn't stop financial experts from presenting estimates of fundamental value. One standard approach is to calculate the "price–earnings (P/E) ratio." This can be done for one company, for all companies in an industry, or for all companies in a composite stock index (such as the Dow or S&P). The P/E ratio is the ratio of a company's stock price to its earnings. The ratio is generally greater than one but can be much greater, even exceeding 100. But, just like stock prices themselves, the P/E ratio is highly volatile, and great caution should be used in using the price–earnings ratio to get a handle on fundamental value.

Why? One reason is that earnings are either past earnings (usually over the previous four quarters of a year) or estimated future earnings. Past earnings might be irrelevant for the fundamental value, and future earnings are unknown and can only be guessed. Also, future earnings must be "discounted" (reduced in value) to convert future earnings to present value (a dollar a year or years from now is worth less than a dollar today)—and it is not clear what interest rate should be used for the discounting. Another reason is that the price of the stock is itself subject to the volatility that has just been discussed. You need to know the price based on fundamental value to construct the P/E ratio to get at fundamental value!

It may be reasonable to conclude that during periods of market stability—meaning steady upward movement—the prices of stocks are close to their fundamental values, whereas during a bubble prices can greatly rise above fundamental values, and during a bubble bursting prices can greatly fall below fundamental values. The implication for rational long-term investment is that stocks should be sold (not bought) during a bubble, and bought (not sold) during a bubble bursting. This "contrarian strategy" is in fact followed by a few (very few) financial firms; but the strategy requires great courage and discipline, as it goes against the instincts of the majority of investors, probably including the investors in these financial firms themselves.

ⓠ What is the difference between stocks and bonds?

ⓐ First, there are some similarities. Both a stock and bond are a security, meaning a document created by one party (the issuer) that provides some rights to the other party (the holder). Both are typically traded in the market; both can have their value go up or down in that market. Both are typically in portfolios of investors. But there the similarity ends. There are differences between stocks and bonds, and these differences can be profound.

A stock, also called a "common stock" or "corporate stock," is a certificate of ownership of a firm. Each stock (also called a "share") represents the holder's share in the equity of the firm (the firm's value after payment of debts and other obligations). Not all firms issue stocks; only corporations do. Obviously, governments cannot issue stock, because their ownership by other parties would violate sovereignty. Stocks connote ownership, and therefore have no maturity date. The stock would cease to exist only if the firm went out of business. If the firm were taken over by another firm or merged with another firm, the stock might be exchanged for the other firm's stock or a newly created firm's stock.

A bond is a certificate of debt. The holder is lending funds to the issuer. Governments, government agencies, and corporations can, and do, issue bonds; but most bonds in existence are central government (in the United States, federal government) bonds. Bonds decidedly have a fixed maturity date, at which time the principal (face value) of the bond is paid off by the issuer and the bond ceases to exist. A 30-year or even a 20-year bond would be considered long-term. There are also short-term bonds, as short as one year.

A bond carries with it a promise to pay interest periodically (for example, semiannually) until the bond matures. The amount of interest (called "coupon interest") is stipulated in the bond and is calculated as the "coupon rate" (meaning the coupon rate of interest) times the face value of the bond. The owner of the bond receives just that amount of interest—no more and no less.

In contrast, stocks have no guaranteed return. While there can be dividends, these are at the discretion of the corporation. However, as the shareholders (owners of stocks) legally own the corporation, there is typically a board of directors elected by stockholders that is supposed to represent their interests. An important function of the board is the hiring of managers to operate the corporation. While there are stockholders' meetings, these are cursory and formalistic affairs. *In practice, individual stockholders have little power to influence the behavior of a firm, even though legally they have all the power.* The only exception is when an individual stockholder has a large share of ownership (10 percent would certainly be considered large). If the firm goes bankrupt, the bondholders are paid off before the stockholders recover any of their equity.

Why hold stocks? Diversification is satisfied when the investor holds both stocks and bonds. Stocks have the advantage of a high potential return, generally through a capital gain—if you are able to sell the stock at a higher price than at which you bought it, or if you can obtain higher valued stock or more stock when there is a merger. Most corporations pay little or no dividends. If a stock does pay regular and substantial dividends, that is also a source of return. But remember that the corporation has no obligation whatsoever to continue to make dividend payments.

Why hold bonds? Bonds are a useful counterweight to stocks, because their interest payments are contractually guaranteed. Also, if the bond is held to maturity, then payment of its principal is also guaranteed. Remember, though, that a corporate bond has a higher risk of default than a government bond. Governments (at least central governments) do not go bankrupt! Both bonds and stocks have a "market risk": If the investor sells them, the price may involve a capital loss or a smaller capital gain than anticipated. But the market risk of bonds is smaller than that of stocks. As the maturity date approaches, the value of the bond typically gets closer to the principal. To compensate, there is the upside of a large capital gain from stocks. Generally, stocks fluctuate in price—both up and down—much more than bonds.

Only the basic types of bonds and stocks have been discussed. There are many variations of each security. Examples follow. "Preferred stock" generally has a dividend guarantee and other benefits as well as deficiencies compared to common stock. Bonds can be zero-coupon (interest implicit in a purchase price lower than face value). Bonds can also be callable, with the issuer having the right to redeem the bonds prior to maturity. That could be disadvantageous to the investor if interest rates have fallen—of course, that is usually the reason that the bonds are called in.

Q What is "the market"?

A "The market" has several meanings. Many people, including economists, use the term to mean "the stock market." Sometimes "the market" is used in an even narrower sense, to refer to the Dow Jones Industrial Average (DJIA), which is the most famous composite index of stock prices. We say "the market went up by 250 points," or the market fell by 3 percent"—implicitly replacing "DJIA" with "the market."

Another meaning is "the market system," denoting the fact that individual consumers (households) and individual producers (firms) make their own economic decisions, guided by prices of commodities that they buy or sell, with these prices determined by the buying and selling decisions of all consumers and producers together. "The market" in that sense is distinct from a "command economy," in which government sets the price of commodities, orders producers what commodities to produce and how much of each commodity, and interferes in the free choice of consumers.

A third meaning of "the market" is any particular market in the economy. For example, people speak of "the market" for automobiles or "the market" for government bonds.

A fourth meaning of "the market" is the market price, whatever it is. If someone complains that the price of an item she wants to buy is too high, or that her salary is too low, you might remark, "That's the market!" Economists use the expression in the same way.

What's the difference between the different markets—for example, NASDAQ, Dow Jones, and the New York Stock Exchange—and where do the commodity markets fit in?

Markets are places where transactions occur. Another way to look at markets is that they are buyers and sellers in their role as actual or potential transactors. A stock market trades stock (of course, of many different companies); a commodity market trades physical commodities (homogeneous products, such as wheat, oil, and gold—homogeneous possibly by specification of a particular grade of quality). Many transactions involve futures contracts, at a price stipulated now but to be carried out at a future date. Also, many such transactions are not consummated by delivery of the stock or commodity, but rather by a settlement in cash via comparison of the new (actual future) price with the contract (predicted future) price.

A market need not be a physical place; the advent of electronic trading involves "virtual" markets, or at least electronic trading in the traditional markets. The market "pit," an area on a particular floor within a stock exchange or commodity exchange building, where potential buyers and sellers (or their representatives) offer to trade and carry out trades, has been largely replaced by the "virtual pit"— electronic trading. There are many markets for stocks (stock exchanges) and commodities (commodity exchanges). Examples of important markets are NASDAQ (National Association of Securities Dealers Automated Quotations), the New York Stock Exchange, and the New York Mercantile Exchange.

Markets should not be confused with indexes of market prices. There are commodity price indexes, which represent prices of a group of commodities (for example, agricultural prices) on a commodities exchange. Stock market indexes represent prices of a group of stocks, and purport to represent the entire market. "Market" has a broad connotation: The stocks need not be all on the same exchange, and the term can refer to all stocks together on all exchanges (at least within the country).

The most famous indexes are the DJIA (Dow Jones Industrial Average, also known as the Dow 30, because the stocks of 30 companies compose the index), the S&P 500 (Standard & Poor's 500), and the NASDAQ composite. Many stocks in the DJIA are not "industrial," or at least are no longer such. The DJIA and S&P 500 involve only a subset of stocks on the New York Stock Exchange. The DJIA is more famous, but the S&P 500 is a broader index. The NASDAQ composite is a rare kind of index, as its components are *all* the stocks listed on the NASDAQ exchange. The NASDAQ is considered an indicator of the movement of the stock prices of technologically oriented companies.

What can create confusion is that there are "index funds," whereby a stock market index is the "asset" traded. Perhaps one should call an index fund a "facsimile asset." Just like ordinary stocks, much trading is on a futures basis ("index futures"). Of course, index fund transactions are always settled in cash; it would be absurd to settle with the large number of securities that comprise the index. The prices of index funds that replicate well-known stock price indexes, such as the S&P 500, are interesting and popular, because of the identification of the overall market movement with the index.

◗ What is "mark to market"?

🅐 "Mark to market," also called "marking to market," assigns the current market price to the value of an asset. If the market price is not known, then an estimate or approximation is used. Mark to market is an accounting rule that is of importance mainly to banks and other financial institutions. The word "mark" in this connotation means a stamp ("mark") of a valuation or price on an asset. "Mark to market" is not the only way of valuing assets on the firm's balance sheet. There are two other ways: "book value" and "mark to model."

Book value, the price at which the asset was acquired, is an alternate valuation scheme. From an economics standpoint, book value is misleading. After all, if you want to sell something that you previously bought, you will get the current market price for it. You can't count on getting the original price. If you paid $100 for something and its market price went down to $60, this means that you can sell it for only $60. It defies both economics and common sense to pretend that it is worth the original $100. Marking to market gives it a price of $60, book valuation assigns a price of $100. Clearly, book value is misleading as a valuation of the asset. Book value does enter into computation of capital gain or loss, which is important for computation of earned income and taxation. In the example above, there is a capital loss of $40.

Another alternative to marking to market is using complicated models to compute the "true" value of an asset or contract, on the grounds that the market value is inappropriate or that there is no market for the item. That technique is sometimes called "mark to model," a takeoff on mark to market. Institutions that invest in complex items, such as mortgage-backed securities and credit default swaps, run the risk of sharp declines in market price, or even no market—that is, no one wanting to buy the items. The bank might complain that the current market price does not take account of the "ultimate" value of the item, which would be much higher. However, economics tells us that prices of financial assets have incorporated in them all information about the future value. The current market price of an asset does incorporate its future value. For example, if it is expected that the asset will go up in price next year, that expectation would be reflected in the current market price and its price would go up right away.

It is unfortunate for a firm that made a bad decision, but the market gives the objective price, and that price could be very low or even zero (no market for the item). Banks that made these unwise investments are prone to say that the market value is inappropriate and therefore that mark to market should not be applied. That justifies a fictitious valuation—a mark to model—that makes the bank's balance sheet seem stronger than it really is.

Conclusion: Mark to market gives the realistic valuation of assets, which is important for rational decision making and economic efficiency.

Q Who manages the infrastructure of electronic banking and information sharing that, for example, allows me to withdraw money from my bank account almost anywhere in the world? Is it decentralized like the Internet? And how vulnerable is it—would it be theoretically possible for some malign entity to delete electronic records of holdings, in the digital equivalent to setting fire to a big pile of cash?

A From the time money was invented, new kinds of money and innovations in ways of transferring money have given rise to concerns. At first, money was only coin. There were no currency bills, no banks, and therefore no deposits and no checks. In colonial times, the principal coin was the Spanish dollar (the forerunner of the U.S. dollar) and its fractional parts. The Spanish dollar was not a bill; it was a silver coin.

For small change, the Spanish dollar was literally cut into as many as eight parts, called "bits" by the colonists. When I was much younger, my friends and I used the expression "two bits" to denote a quarter. I did not know it then, but now I know—and so do you—that "two bits" were two-eighths, or one-quarter, of the Spanish dollar. It is amazing that the slang persisted over several centuries.

In cutting the Spanish dollar into "bits," and even without breaking up the coin, unscrupulous colonists would engage in the practices of "clipping" and "sweating," which were techniques of obtaining some of the valuable silver metal from the coin. Then they would put the coin back into circulation at face value, by buying something with it. If a coin became too light, it might be accepted only at less than face value. So you were taking a risk in getting a coin, not knowing if it was lighter than full weight. The same problem applied to the other coins in circulation. Note that the danger was not the counterfeiting of coins, which was difficult and expensive to do, but rather the unnatural lightness of the coins.

Then paper money was invented, also in colonial times, beginning in the colony of Massachusetts. With paper money (currency bills), counterfeiting became profitable and was prevalent. People were suspicious of bills because they could never be sure whether they were counterfeit and therefore could be rejected as payment to another party. Of course, modern techniques of making bills "counterfeit proof" did not exist at that time; but, even today, counterfeit bills do circulate on occasion.

When banks came into the picture, deposits and checks, which were used to transfer deposits, were introduced. Checks are not money; rather, they are used to transfer money from one person's account to another's. People worried that their checks could be stolen, their signature forged, or the original amount on the check changed to one much higher. Another concern was that the bank could make a mistake in their deposit account, to their disadvantage—it could be unintentional, even a simple clerical error.

With electronic banking, there are new fears. Thus far at least, electronic banking does not involve the creation of new money. Rather, it is a means of moving money at lightning speed, even around the world, as you properly stated. Yes, electronic banking is essentially decentralized, and largely operates via the Internet. No one manages the Internet overall. If there were such a manager, then we would not be suffering from the deluge of spam! The greatest danger is that you yourself make a mistake by entering the wrong amount on the keyboard. (That is also true for ATMs, automatic teller machines, which do *not* operate via the Internet.) But that kind of error is much less likely to happen when checks are used, because the process of writing a check takes time.

Now consider your fear that a malevolent entity could enter your bank via the Internet and transfer money from your deposit account to her own account elsewhere, even halfway around the world. Financial institutions make use of computer technology to guard against that occurrence. In fact, banks take tremendous care to make sure that fears such as yours do not become reality. Why? Because then the banks would suffer tremendous bad publicity, and would lose their customers. Yes, what you worry about is theoretically possible; but, as a realistic event, it is extremely unlikely.

Q It makes me nervous to see banks advertising so much. It means they're not paying enough interest on the money—my money—that they're holding. Why doesn't the government pass laws to make the banks pay higher returns?

A Banks advertise for the same reason that other businesses advertise: to get more customers. In general, if advertising were not permitted, many new products and new services would not make it in the marketplace. Advertising attracts more customers (borrowers and depositors) to your bank. With a large customer base, the bank can realize "economies of scale" (spreading its costs among more customers) and therefore provide its services more cheaply. True, some advertising is negative and misleading; but that is unlikely to be true for banking, which is a competitive industry. If your bank misled people, it would rapidly lose credibility, lose existing customers, and not get new customers. If banks could increase their profits by advertising less and paying higher interest rates instead, they would do so—and some might already be doing so! Chances are, however, that the typical bank's advertising budget is not large enough to make a measurable difference to the interest rates that it offers on deposits.

Your idea that the government should pass laws to force banks to pay higher interest rates would be opposed by almost all economists. Banks would not be able to do that unless they received higher interest rates on their loans and securities portfolios. Interest rates are determined in highly competitive markets. To compel banks to go against market interest rates would force some to go out of business and others to have reduced profits, resulting in less expansion and reduced services or higher fees for services. And equity considerations would extend the government control of interest rates to other financial institutions as well. The outcome would be substantial economic inefficiency.

Q Why are commercial banks classified differently from investment banks?

A The reason is historical. Commercial banks accept deposits, make loans, and buy securities. Investment banks underwrite securities (meaning they purchase and resell new issues of stocks and bonds) and provide general financial advice (including advice on mergers with, or acquisitions of, other companies) and financial services to corporations and governments. Investment banks also create mortgage-backed securities (MBSs, called "securitizing mortgages"). Commercial banks have the opportunity of borrowing funds from the central bank (the Federal Reserve), whereas, up until 2008, investment banks were not permitted to do so.

Until 1999, U.S. law prevented commercial banks and investment banks from having the same ownership. That is no longer true, and a single organization can now have separate commercial-banking and investment-banking components.

Q **How does it benefit banks to foreclose on homes that they can't sell?**

A Any property can be sold if the price is low enough. So the bank can always recoup *some* of its investment. It may be that the bank *expected* that the home would be auctioned at a price at least equal to the remaining principal in the mortgage, but the housing market worsened in the interim. Sometimes it can take a long time until the foreclosure process is completed, which increases the risk to the bank that foreclosed.

Another possibility is that the bank wants to set an example. If it lets one borrower get away with violating terms of the mortgage, other borrowers may expect the same treatment. Banks (in this case, acting as mortgage lenders, called mortgagees) want borrowers (in this case, called mortgagors, those who took out the mortgages) to focus first on payment of interest and repayment of principal. They want borrowers to cut back on all spending and all other repayment of debt and pay off the mortgage according to contract. Alleviation of mortgage conditions gets borrowers off the hook in first paying off their mortgage obligations.

It is also true that banks could benefit from giving a borrower temporary relief, especially if there is strong evidence that the borrower will improve her financial situation in the near future and be able to meet the mortgage conditions in full, even compensating the bank for the relief. Also, there are costs to foreclosure (both money costs and inconvenience), which banks could avoid by seeking alternatives that allow borrowers to remain in their homes and improve their financial situation.

From the standpoint both of rational decision making and of economic efficiency, the bank should make its own decision on whether to play "hardball" (foreclosure) or "softball" (breaks to homeowners close to, or in, foreclosure). If the government uses persuasion or legislation to induce the bank to play softball, the bank could be doing what it otherwise would choose not to do; the result could be inefficient. If the breaks to homeowners are financed by the government, the banks might agree and even be pleased—but now taxpayers are paying for homeowners' debts. There is not only economic inefficiency but also unfairness. Why should taxpayers pay for the consequences of decisions made by lenders and borrowers?

Q What are hedge funds, and why are they so mysterious? Can I be hurt if a hedge fund goes under, even if I don't participate in hedge-fund investing?

A Hedge funds are a type of investment fund; that is, they acquire money from investors (individuals and institutions) and seek to profit from investment. They are atypical funds (in particular, unlike mutual funds) in several ways. First, hedge funds are not required to register with the Securities and Exchange Commission (SEC), the government agency that regulates the securities industry, and also are not required to make periodic reports to that body. That lack of required disclosure makes hedge funds secretive or, at least, less transparent than mutual funds.

Second, and a primary reason for the nonrequirements, hedge funds have small numbers of investors and/or are restricted to wealthy investors, within the limitations specified by U.S. law. The presumption is that only wealthy and well-informed people invest in hedge funds, and that such people do not need the protection of the SEC. Again, small numbers and wealthy investors add to the mystery of hedge funds.

Third, hedge funds can undertake a wide range of investment activity, both in outlets and in methods. They can (1) engage in heavy leveraging (investing a large multiple of borrowed funds), so that even a low return per dollar invested results in a high total return; and (2) invest in ultra-risky assets, in the hope of a high return per dollar.

Fourth, the reason for those practices is that management fees are much higher in hedge funds than in mutual funds. Typically, there is not only an "asset management fee" of 1 or 2 percent of assets (itself on the high range of similar fees for mutual funds) but also a "performance fee" around 20 percent, although the performance fee can be lower or even higher. Clearly, management has a huge potential reward via risk taking. Management gains tremendously if the risky investment pays off, but does not lose anything (beyond less assets upon which the asset management fee is assessed) if the risky investment fails.

Fifth, hedge funds generally have restrictions on redemptions of shares (cashing in all or part of your investment in the fund). Redemption can be limited to only a few times a year, and your investment in the fund could be made unavailable ("frozen") for a long period of time (even a year or more).

In sum, hedge funds are a most unwise investment outlet for almost all people and institutions. An exception could be wealthy individuals who welcome the chance of a large profit even with the associated disadvantage of a large risk of losing their investment. Another exception could be institutions that view a "high-reward, high-risk" investment as part of an overall diversification investment strategy in which most other investment is "low-reward, low-risk."

I don't see how you could be hurt directly if a hedge fund fails, providing, of course, that you—and people you care about, and institutions in which you have an interest, such as your pension fund—are not among the investors in the fund. Indirectly, you may be hurt if the investors in the fund are your clients or customers of the firm where you work. It is also possible that the failure of the hedge fund is part of a series of failures of financial institutions (what economists call a "systemic" failure), but that situation would be no different from the failure of a bank or indeed a mutual fund.

Q What is a mortgage-backed security?

A Think of a mortgage-backed security (MBS) as a bond mutual fund. Just like a bond, an MBS is a debt obligation that entitles the holder to earnings (the principal and interest on the underlying mortgages) in proportion to its shares in the MBS. Both government agencies (Ginnie Mae) and government-sponsored institutions (Fannie

Mae and Freddie Mac) and private financial institutions (such as investment banks) create MBSs by purchasing mortgages from originators (lenders, called "mortgagees") and assembling the mortgages into a pool. Thus the term "securitization" (of the mortgages). Gone are the days when a mortgage was a simple affair: you and your lending institution (savings and loan association or commercial bank).

Things are even more complicated because there are several types of MBSs, depending on the property (residential or commercial) mortgaged, the type of earnings (principal and interest together, principal alone, interest alone), and priority of payment (equal for all holders of the MBS, separated according to maturity or other quality). The different kinds of MBSs each have their own special name. The names that I like best include the adjective "stripped," as the interest or principal are "stripped off" and securitized separately.

When things become more complicated, they can become more dangerous. When MBSs were originated, it was thought that they had the advantage of diversification, so that if one mortgagor (borrower) failed to pay on time, or even defaulted, the inclusion of only bits of hundreds or thousands of mortgages into one security would provide protection for the investors in MBSs. The development of a secondary market, so that investors in MBSs could sell them to others—thus spreading any risk among more institutions—was also considered beneficial. So was the creation of insurance contracts (credit default swaps, CDSs) in which (in this case) an investor could purchase the right to be paid if an MBS goes into default. To make matters even more unreal, the seller and purchaser of the CDS could have nothing to do with the MBS or even the underlying mortgages; they could be third (even fourth and fifth) parties.

So we have a situation in which a mass of securities and contracts are superimposed on a much lower value of mortgages and underlying property (real estate). Diversification is of little use if a substantial number of mortgagees default. And if, as a consequence, the MBSs issuers cannot make payment, insurance contracts must be paid off. If the sellers of the CDSs are leveraged (have ready funds to pay off only a small proportion of the insured MBSs), then a "financial meltdown" is a possibility. This can happen even though intentions were good: Spread the risk.

One can argue that the problem begins at the bottom end: the original mortgages, when homeowners took on obligations that they could not honor over time. One could just as well claim the problem is at the top end: the leveraging associated with CDSs. The government is not blameless in this situation. Note that government and quasi-government agencies named in the first paragraph are heavily involved in the creation of MBSs (though not CDSs). More transparency and oversight (and possibly regulation) would obviously be useful for transactions in MBSs and CDSs. Those in the market for these instruments would make better decisions for themselves and for the entire financial sector if all transactions were reported to a central body and in the public domain, with overall statistics (of transaction prices, and of security and contract characteristics) computed and released quickly and regularly. Greater involvement of the Securities and Exchange Commission (SEC) and other government agencies could be the mechanism to do this.

Q What are interest rates? How and why do they change?

A An interest rate is the price for the use of funds. The rate is expressed as a percentage of the amount transacted and per time period (usually per year—even if the interest is paid at another frequency; for example, monthly). The borrower receives the funds so that she can make purchases in the present; the lender provides the funds so that she will have more funds (principal plus interest accumulation) in the future.

So interest rates play an important role in the economy. They provide compensation so that individuals, businesses, and governments can trade present and future purchasing power. Lenders are savers; they give up present purchasing power for the future. Borrowers are spenders; they obtain more present purchasing power than their current income permits. Without interest, there would be very little lending and borrowing, and therefore only small amounts of saving and investment. The economy would grow more slowly, if at all.

Even though economists simplify by speaking of "the interest rate," in fact there are many different interest rates in the economy and many different instruments (called "debt instruments") that carry with them an interest rate. When you put money in a bank account that pays interest, you are lending to the bank (the bank is borrowing from you). When you buy a government bond, you are lending funds to the government (the government is borrowing funds from you). And, obviously, when you borrow money from a bank, the bank is lending to you. Banks also lend to and borrow from each other, as well as borrow from the central bank; businesses and governments borrow from banks; and so on.

Interest rates differ according to (1) the credit-worthiness of the borrower (the higher the probability of default, the borrower not paying back, the higher is the interest rate to compensate); (2) the term to maturity (the longer the funds are borrowed, usually the higher the interest rate); and (3) the type of debt instrument (the more negotiable—easily transferable—the debt, the lower the interest rate). Interest rates are highly dependent on expectations. If it is generally expected that there will be higher inflation in the future, then interest rates will go up; lenders will insist on compensation for being repaid in dollars that will be worth less in purchasing power than the dollars that they lend. They will get that compensation, because otherwise they will not lend.

Most interest rates move together. Like most other prices, interest rates are determined in a market. The forces that change interest rates in general are demand and supply. Therefore interest rates change according to market forces. If there are more funds available for lending (for example, because foreigners are investing in our country), then interest rates fall. If the economy is booming, then households and businesses want to borrow more to finance expenditures, and interest rates go up.

To repeat, interest rates are determined in markets. If any lender insists on a higher interest rate than the market (after taking account of special factors, such as credit-worthiness of the borrower), the lender will not be able to make loans. If a borrower insists on a lower interest rate than market, the borrower will not be able to get a loan.

Q What is a "financial panic"?

A The word "panic" means an excessive state of alarm or fear that leads to irrational behavior. A financial panic is generally a banking panic, and it differs from panic in general in that it is widespread, not confined to one individual or entity.

The panic can be either liquidity-type or solvency-type. A liquidity-type panic is a run on banks. Depositors rush to take their money out of banks, for fear the bank will fail or at the least close its doors temporarily, preventing cash withdrawals for a period of time. This panic feeds on itself. A solvency-based panic involves loans going bad. Banks fear that their loans will not be repaid, call in their loans, and refuse to lend. The danger to the banks is that their assets will fall and bankruptcy will loom. Again the panic feeds on itself.

How realistic is each form of panic today? With government-guaranteed deposit insurance, runs on banks would appear to be a thing of the past. But that is an exaggeration. Some banks do not have deposit insurance. In that situation, fears of depositors that their deposits may be uncashable could be rational, and runs could happen. Even a bank with deposit insurance might suffer a run, because depositors could be worried that time could elapse before they are paid, or that the process of receiving the cash could be inconvenient.

The fear that a bank lacks sufficient cash in its vault to pay off all depositors at once is based on reality. Even if the vault cash is supplemented by the bank's deposits at the Fed, the cash would be insufficient. No bank could be profitable if it held 100 percent of its deposit liabilities in the form of reserves. It is the making of loans and purchase of securities that give rise to bank profits. Bank income-earning assets (loans and securities) are largely long-term, while bank liabilities (deposits) are largely short-term. That is why even the best-managed banks cannot *quickly* assemble cash to pay off *all or a large part* of their deposits. So, without deposit insurance, a liquidity-type panic would bring down even solvent banks (banks that are in no danger of bankruptcy).

A solvency-type panic is of two types. First, banks fear that their business and consumer borrowers will be unable to repay their loans. That can have a devastating effect on the bank's balance sheet and cause the institution to become insolvent. Even as some loans are repaid, the banks may refuse to make new loans. Second, banks (or financial institutions in general) fear that the loans they make to one another will not be repaid, or the contracts they transact with one another will not be honored. Then the lending that financial institutions make to one another dries up. It is entirely possible that both solvency-type panics occur simultaneously.

Solvency-type panics are not as easy for the government to prevent as liquidity-type panics. One policy would be for the government to guarantee loans that banks make to the public and/or to guarantee loans that the banks make to one another. That policy would create a "moral hazard" problem, meaning that it would destroy the incentive of banks to make sound lending decisions and to avoid risk uncompensated by a higher expected return. Why not lend to high-risk borrowers and take out high-risk contracts, for a higher expected return, if any losses on these contracts will be covered by the government?

Q Why was deregulation of the financial industry so firmly sought by the U.S. government? Could this deregulation be the cause of any recession that followed?

A The government pushed Congress for legislation to deregulate the financial industry because of the increased competition and enhanced efficiency that would ensue. Deregulation permitted banks to charge any interest rates that they wanted on deposits, treated credit unions and savings and loans associations essentially the same as banks, and permitted banks to offer commercial banking services, investment banking services, and insurance services. As a consequence, mergers of commercial banks and financial banks could readily occur. Removal of restrictions on the free market typically enhances economic efficiency.

It is hard to believe that financial deregulation in itself could be the cause of a recession. With financial efficiency enhanced, the flow of funds from savers (lenders) to spenders and investors (borrowers) occurs at lower cost and with less friction. However, one could argue that deregulation fosters unwarranted lending to borrowers who were not creditworthy. This could set up an economic expansion that would be replaced by a recession when the boom collapsed. That argument says that the free market, brought about by deregulation, doesn't work properly in the financial sector.

The free market does not seem to be working properly when complex assets, such as mortgage-backed securities, are purchased by buyers who are unaware of the risks involved or believe that they can adequately insure the risks, and when contracts on borrowers defaulting turn into bets on whether or not borrowers will default. The financial sectors' function of intermediation between borrowers and lenders turns into a game of musical chairs: Who is left holding the bad assets and bad contracts? The problem is that the chairs are semi-attached, and a few chairs falling can bring down the lot of them.

However, the cause of a subsequent recession is not deregulation in itself, but rather poor management and horrible decision making. A free market does not guarantee profits. It offers enhanced scope for either profits or losses, depending on the decisions taken.

Chapter 7

CYCLES AND GROWTH (BOOMS AND BUSTS)

Now we come to the big national picture. In this chapter, *Everyday Economics* explains the workings of the overall economy, what economists love to call the "macroeconomy." Okay, you can't influence the macroeconomy, at least not by yourself alone. But a lot of people and a lot of businesses acting together affect the macroeconomy. Something else is clear: the macroeconomy certainly affects you in important ways: whether or not you have an ongoing job; the general standard of living of the country; the amount of inflation (which is the increase in the prices that you pay for commodities in general); and so on.

◉ What is per-capita GDP, and why is it important?

Ⓐ GDP, short for "gross domestic product," denotes the total production of goods and services within a country during a given time period, generally a quarter year or a full year. How can we add up amounts of different commodities produced? (You can't "add" 25 million personal computers and 700 million bushels of apples.) The technique is to multiply ("weight") the quantity of each commodity by the price of the commodity. (So, if personal computers have an average price of $1,000 and apples are $10 a bushel, the addition of $25 billion plus $7 billion, equaling $32 billion, is legitimate.) In that way, the country's total production is obtained on a consistent basis.

For a true measure of output over time, we need to correct GDP for inflation. If GDP is not so corrected, it is called "nominal GDP" (or "money GDP"). If GDP is so corrected, it is termed "real GDP" (or "deflated GDP"). Real GDP is obtained by dividing nominal GDP by a price index, called the "GDP deflator." The GDP deflator encompasses changes in the prices of *all* components of output—consumer goods and services; goods purchased by business (investment goods); and government production of, and spending on, goods and services. The GDP deflator is a measure of how prices in general, or on average, have changed. If money GDP increases by 8 percent over a previous year but prices are higher by 3 percent, then real GDP goes up by only about 5 percent.

Real GDP is important, because it measures how the overall economy is doing. Many economists consider it a recession if there are two successive quarters of reduction in real GDP (for example, real GDP falling from $14.3 to $13.8 to $13.1 trillion, at annual rates, over three quarters). This reduction in real GDP would mean that more people are becoming unemployed. In the other direction, if real GDP goes up at a rapid rate, then unemployment is falling substantially.

Per-capita nominal GDP is of little interest; but per-capita real GDP has an important meaning. To obtain per-capita real GDP, simply divide real GDP by population. So per-capita real GDP is each person's average share of real GDP. Per-capita real GDP measures how fast the country's output is growing in proportion to its population. It is the best indicator of the country's economic growth. If per-capita real GDP goes up, then there are more goods and services potentially available to each consumer—only potentially, because the increased output can take the form of business investment or government goods and services or exports net of imports. While the standard of living of the population may not actually increase, certainly the potential has gone up. And, in the long run, standard of living will move up with per-capita real GDP.

Ⓠ What are economic cycles? Why do they happen? Is there a way to stop them?

Ⓐ The usual term for "economic cycle" is "business cycle" or simply "the cycle." But the term "economic cycle" or "economic fluctuation" is more descriptive, because the business cycle is defined in terms of the behavior of real GDP (gross domestic product—the economy's total output of goods and services—corrected for inflation, so it is GDP in "real" terms, as if total output were a physical amount of one commodity). Still, the term "business cycle" is so prevalent that we use it here.

GDP has a certain trend growth. That might be 3 percent a year. This means that, *on average,* GDP ("trend GDP") goes up by 3 percent a year. Why? Because the economy's resources—the workforce, human capital (training and education embodied in the workforce), and physical capital (factories, office buildings, machinery, and equipment)—on average go up year after year, and the level of technology (ways to make existing products and the creation of new products) also improves over time. The expansion of resources and the improvement in technology would generate real GDP increasing *on average* by the 3 percent mentioned.

But *actual* GDP is not necessarily the same as trend GDP. GDP can increase more than 3 percent or less than 3 percent. In fact, GDP can even decrease. The fluctuation of actual GDP around trend GDP is the business cycle. Commonly, one thinks of a cycle as having a certain regularity or recurrence. But that is not true in reality—at least it is not true for the business cycle. Some cycles are short, some are long. Some entail large deviations from trend GDP, some involve short deviations.

When actual GDP is above trend GDP, the economy is in the expansionary phase of the cycle. When actual GDP is below trend GDP, the economy is in the contractionary phase. Really high actual GDP compared to trend GDP is sometimes called an "overheated" economy. Really low actual GDP compared to trend GDP is called a "recession." And critically low actual GDP would mark a "depression." (Remember that both actual GDP and trend GDP refer to real GDP.)

You might ask how the business cycle affects you. Real GDP (I am emphasizing the "real" here) carries employment with it. Think of the situation as economists do. Instead of employment, consider its reverse: unemployment. If GDP falls, unemployment rises; if GDP rises, unemployment falls. So the business cycle, defined as the behavior of GDP, carries with it an unemployment cycle. People find it hard to get a first job or a new job in a recession, but easier to find jobs in an expansion. In an overheated economy, there is substantial inflation, which hurts people living on a fixed income or on income that does not increase as much as prices do.

Why do business cycles happen? Economists have a lot of ideas on the subject, but there is no consensus. To ask why business cycles happen is also to ask: Why can't actual GDP be trend GDP all the time? In other words, why can't actual GDP be identical to trend GDP year after year, with the consequence of no business cycle?

It doesn't happen for at least three reasons. *First,* the economy encounters "shocks," which immediately make it impossible for actual GDP to be identical to trend GDP. A shock is an unexpected, sudden, temporary event that shakes up the economy. A good example is an oil price increase or an oil price decrease. Another example is a sudden or unexpected increase or decrease in stock market prices. Finally, there could be a natural or other disaster, such as a serious hurricane or another 9/11 terrorist attack.

The immediate consequence of the shock is an upward or downward movement in actual GDP. The question becomes why isn't there an immediate, or a quick, return to trend GDP. The answer (and the *second* reason why actual GDP doesn't stay even with trend GDP) is that people and businesses just don't behave that way. They adjust slowly even to a sudden change in circumstance. Businesses see their costs go up when the price of energy unexpectedly jumps. They don't increase their prices to compensate, at least not right away. And if they do increase prices, sales go down. Either way, the businesses reduce their production, and layoff or fire workers.

Another example: Individuals feel richer when their stock prices suddenly go up. But they don't increase spending immediately in the amount in which their stocks went up, and then bring their spending back down again quickly (commensurate with the fall of the stock price). Instead, they spread out their spending increase over time. This "smoothing behavior" is human nature, and therefore, business nature and consumer nature.

The *third* reason for actual GDP staying away from trend GDP is that the people and businesses in the economy naturally have "waves of optimism and pessimism." People spend more money and businesses hire more workers and expand operations when they are optimistic about the future of the economy, and do the opposite when they are pessimistic. Note that the optimism or pessimism can be a consequence as well as a cause of the business cycle. In other words, that attitude can jump-start the cycle and/or make it stronger.

Can business cycles be stopped? Governments and central banks try. They have not yet succeeded, and probably never will. There are several reasons. First, it is usually not obvious, and in fact quite controversial, whether or not the economy *is* in a recession and whether or not it *is* in an expansion. It is even harder to predict whether the economy is *about to be* in one of these phases. Second, there must be political or administrative agreement among government (or central bank) decision makers about what action to take, and how much action.

Third, the action taken has effects on the economy that cannot be predicted either in timing or in strength. To fight a recession, policymakers can use monetary policy (lowering interest rates, increasing the reserves and lending ability of banks) or fiscal policy (lowering taxes or increasing government spending). These policies can actually worsen the economic cycle. Just at the time when the policy is most effective, the economy could be changing, or have already changed, from recession to expansion—and then the economy would overheat. The opposite can happen as well, with government action to fight an overheated economy exacerbating a recession.

To summarize, we sort of understand the nature of the business cycle—but we can't predict it and don't yet know how to stop the cycle or even how to moderate it. That doesn't stop government from trying to do so—sometimes worsening the cycle in the process.

Ⓠ Can the government turn around a downward economic cycle? How?

Ⓐ The government can certainly *try* to turn around a recession (short for "downward economic cycle"); but whether it will succeed is problematic. The government policies used to do so are expansionary fiscal policy (a deliberate budget deficit) and expansionary monetary policy (the Federal Reserve [Fed] buying government bonds in the open market, thus increasing bank reserves). There are reasons why each policy may not work. The increased government spending may "crowd out" private spending, because government borrowing to finance the budget deficit drives up interest rates and discourages business borrowing to finance investment and consumer borrowing to finance spending. The Fed action directly increases only bank reserves, and the banks may decide not to lend.

Also, even if the policies are effective, they may be effective at the wrong time. Both monetary and fiscal policy take time to work. It could be that, by the time the monetary and fiscal policies have their impact, the economy has naturally turned around and is in the expansionary phase of an economic cycle. Now, instead of fighting a recession, the policies make the economy overheat, and inflation results.

But it is very possible that the policies are ineffective, at least as far as increasing private spending on goods and services, which the economy and individual businesses need in a recession. Both individuals and businesses can be pessimistic about the future of the economy when there is a recession. Indeed, that pessimism could have caused the recession. When individuals are afraid of losing jobs, they spend less. When businesses worry that their sales will be off, they stop hiring new workers. When financial institutions fear that their loans will not be paid back, they stop making new loans. The financial institutions may even be afraid of lending to each other.

One of the most difficult things to do is to end a general pessimistic outlook about the economy. If the government just says that there is no reason to be pessimistic, that tactic may backfire and pessimism becomes panic: People think that only a dire situation would cause the government to make a statement like that!

Eventually the economy will correct itself. A recession means more unemployment and therefore less upward pressure on wages (less wage increases, and even wage decreases), which reduces costs for businesses. Both lower costs and the recession itself reduce prices or inflation, and enhance the purchasing power of money and other assets, which increases spending. As sales increase, the economy turns around and the recession ends. This corrective process will work, but might take a long time.

The government can help by reducing rigidities in the economy, which tend to keep costs up. One example is the minimum wage, which prevents wages from falling below a government-specified hourly rate. Another example is restrictive work rules (adopted in negotiations with unions) that prevent firms from adopting the cheapest way of increasing production.

Q What is "stagflation"? How does it relate to recession and inflation?

A "Stagflation" involves both recession and inflation. Stagflation is a combination of stagnation (meaning a prolonged recession) and substantial inflation. At one time it was believed that substantial inflation could not exist in a recession. The idea was that, as the economy moved further into a recession, businesses would fire more workers and have more plants idle. Also, they would accumulate more and more inventories that were unplanned, as sales fell short of expectations. Therefore, upward pressure on wages and prices would weaken substantially, and inflation would fall to a low level.

Then economists came to realize that the behavior of labor during a recession needed to be incorporated. Workers, particularly when represented by unions, are very reluctant to accept decreases in wages at any time, including during a recession. Even when prices are rising very little, workers will try to achieve substantial wage increases, though perhaps not as much as they would under substantial inflation. The result is "wage-push inflation." Over time, with wages increasing as much as price increases during high inflation and wages increasing more than price increases during low inflation, the inflation rate at a given unemployment rate (or at a given stage in a recession) goes up. Wage push is stronger in forcing inflation up than are idle plants in forcing inflation down.

Still later, and continuing to the present, economists have changed their minds again. Economists observed that, at least in the private sector, the percentage of workers in unions has fallen dramatically. They also see that, largely as a result, businesses offering low, if any, wage increases during a recession get away with it; workers accept the terms, because they are afraid of losing their jobs. So economists have largely lost interest in stagflation as an interesting phenomenon to be studied. Indeed, it is thought that price deflation (the opposite of price inflation—prices falling by a certain percent every year) could actually happen during a recession. That would be the very opposite of the inflation component of stagflation.

Q What is the difference between a recession and a depression?

A A standard economics joke goes as follows: "A recession is when other people are unemployed. A depression is when you are unemployed." There is some truth in the statement. A depression is simply a serious and prolonged recession. More people are unemployed, and for longer periods, in a depression.

But there is some unfortunate nastiness in the joke, because the suggestion is that economists believe that people are always and totally selfish—with each person caring only about himself or herself and not at all about other people. That is not what economists believe. Just because you are concerned with what is best for you (which admittedly is an assumption that economists often make) does not mean that you don't care about other folks or about the country or about the world.

Could the world ever again suffer a depression such as happened in the 1930s?

It is extremely unlikely that the world would ever again suffer a depression as happened in the 1930s. The "Great Depression" of the 1930s took place because of events that could not possibly recur. A tremendous number of banks failed, largely because of "runs on banks," as people rushed to get their deposits out in cash. There was no government-insured deposit insurance as there is today. There was the gold standard, which limited the ability of banks to increase the money supply; there is no gold standard today. It was unclear then how monetary policy and fiscal policy would work to prevent or alleviate the depression; today we have much greater knowledge of how these policies work. The problem was a lack of spending (not enough demand for goods and services), and the government did not help much.

Nevertheless, it remains true today, as it was in the 1930s, that deep and widespread pessimism about the future of the economy could bring about or aggravate a recession. Whether it could turn the recession into a serious and prolonged recession, which we call a depression, is still unlikely. The problem is that banks cannot be forced to lend money, even if the central bank provides them with the means (more bank reserves) to do so. If the banks are not confident of being repaid, they won't make loans. That could certainly bring about a recession, even a serious recession. Through open-market purchase of bonds, the central bank could keep on increasing bank reserves and the liquidity of banks, and pushing down interest rates; but nothing else happens if the banks do not lend.

In that situation, expansionary fiscal policy could take over: reduction of taxes and increase in government spending. Even though people might initially be too pessimistic to spend their increased after-tax income, eventually they will do so if taxes are cut enough. The increased government spending on commodities will also induce businesses to increase production. Eventually, banks will see the profit in making loans. Pessimism on the part of all concerned will change to optimism, and the economy will move out of the recession.

To fully answer your question, there is the possibility that a depression of the caliber of the 1930s could again recur; but, unlike the 1930s, the cause would be on the supply side. If a large portion of productive capacity (physical capital, such as factories, machinery, and equipment, and infrastructure, such as roads, bridges, and airports) were wiped out by war, civil strife, or natural disaster (such as a tremendous meteor hitting the country), then a depression would result. The solution to that kind of depression would be physical in addition to financial (monetary or fiscal policy). The infrastructure would have to be rebuilt and the physical capital re-accumulated. That seems like a near-impossible task, but Germany and Japan did it after World War II.

Q How does consumer confidence factor into economic outcome?

A To judge by the number of indexes of consumer confidence that are regularly published, many observers believe in the importance of consumer confidence to the economy. Consumers are asked for their views on their own future employment and financial situations, on their planned purchases, and for their impressions of the future of the overall economy. An interesting question without a known answer is the extent to which economic decisions of business and government are influenced by the published consumer-confidence measures.

Unquestionably, consumer confidence is important to the economy. If individuals are scared about their employment or fearful of the stability of their finances, they are likely not to spend as much. That translates into less consumer spending on goods and services, which means less revenue and lower profits for business, as well as reduced business investment in physical plant and inventories. Substantial unemployment naturally results.

Similarly, if people believe that the stock market will fall, that in itself could bring about a fall in stock prices—because the very lack of confidence is reflected in panic sales of stocks. When there is a financial crisis, the pessimistic outlook on the economy could be shared by businesses, and a severe financial panic both results from and adds to the pessimism. There could just as well be consumer (and business) optimism, with beneficial results for both financial markets and the real economy.

Some economists believe that waves of optimism and pessimism are characteristic of the stock market, making the market go up and down cyclically, with similar implications for the economy. Ironically, general pessimism might occur simply because of the general belief that there is general pessimism. The same applies to general optimism. The views of one of the greatest economists of all time, though written long ago, hold true today:

> Day-to-day fluctuations in the profits of existing investments, which are obviously of an ephemeral and non-significant character, tend to have an altogether excessive, and even an absurd, influence on the market. . . . In one of the greatest investment markets in the world, namely, New York, the influence of speculation . . . is enormous. Even outside the field of finance, Americans are apt to be unduly interested in discovering what average opinion believes average opinion to be; and this national weakness finds its nemesis in the stock market. . . .
>
> Even apart from the instability due to speculation, there is the instability due to the characteristic of human nature that a large proportion of our positive activities depend[s] on spontaneous optimism rather than on a mathematical expression, whether moral or hedonistic or economic . . .

This means, unfortunately, not only that slumps and depressions are exaggerated in degree, but that economic prosperity is excessively dependent on a political and social atmosphere which is congenial to the average business man.*

Q Under normal economic conditions, why does inflation inevitably occur?

A Inflation is the percentage increase in the general price level—for example, 5 percent per year, meaning that prices in general go up by 5 percent every year or possibly 5 percent in this year compared to last year. Inflation may not be uniform. Some prices may go up by less than 5 percent, or even fall, while other prices go up by more than 5 percent.

The most commonsense explanation that economists have for inflation is in the famous expression "inflation is too much money chasing too few goods," meaning goods and services ("commodities"). Money gives households, firms, and governments immediate purchasing power. The greater the increase in the money supply, or in its rate of growth, the greater that purchasing power. Of course, the greater, too, is inflation, except that there is another item in the statement: the amount of commodities that is produced. With more things to buy, money gains purchasing power. The greater the amount of goods and services produced, or the greater the rate of growth of that amount, the less the inflation.

The money-supply increase is usually expressed as a "rate of growth," because production of goods and services naturally has a trend increase (say, 3 percent per year), due to improvements in technology, expansion of the workforce, and increase in physical capital (factories, office buildings, machinery, and equipment). So an increase in money would affect inflation only if it exceeded that trend increase (3 percent per year).

---

* John Maynard Keynes, *The General Theory of Employment, Interest and Money*. London: Macmillan, 1936, pp. 153–154, 158–159, 161, 162. Reproduced with permission of Palgrave Macmillan.

Some economists, called "monetarists," believe that inflation can result *only* from too much increase in the money supply or its rate of growth. That makes a lot of sense when the government or central bank prints money like mad and "hyperinflation"—inflation that gets larger and larger—results. But, under normal economic conditions, the increased money supply would also act to increase production of commodities. The end result could be either increased or decreased inflation.

Who is hurt by inflation? Does anyone gain?

Lenders are hurt by inflation, because they are paid back in dollars worth less in terms of commodities. Workers also are hurt, because they accepted wages on the assumption that there would no inflation or less inflation than actually occurred. Borrowers gain, because they pay their debt in dollars worth less than what they borrowed. Businesses gain, because their prices go up more than the wages they pay. The only way for there to be no gainers or losers is for the inflation to be generally and correctly anticipated, so that interest rates go by the amount of inflation and wages go up as much as prices.

People on fixed income such as pensions are unambiguously hurt by inflation, because their pensions are the same dollar amount but that amount buys less commodities.

What is deflation?

Deflation is the exact opposite of inflation. A 2-percent deflation means a fall in the general price level by 2 percent per year or 2 percent in this year compared to last year. The fall need not be uniform; some prices may go down by more than 2 percent, some by less. The cause of a deflation is not enough money for too many goods. To reduce output might end the deflation but at the expense of more unemployment. A better solution is for the central bank to increase the money supply or its rate of growth.

Who is hurt by deflation, and who gains?

Lenders and workers gain from deflation that takes everyone by surprise. The lenders get paid back in dollars worth more in terms of commodities, and the workers enjoy a greater purchasing power of their wages. Borrowers lose, because they pay their loans back in dollars worth more than when they borrowed. Firms lose, because they get lower prices than they expected for the commodities that they produce. Fixed-income pensioners gain, because their fixed dollar income buys more commodities. If the deflation is anticipated, it will be reflected in lower interest rates and lower wages. Then no one gains or loses, except those on fixed incomes.

Since the 1930s, there has been a lot of inflation in countries such as the United States but, with rare exception, no deflation. It is likely that modern central banks would increase the money supply substantially in order to avoid deflation.

Does lowering interest rates prove to stimulate growth? Why?

Lower interest rates reduce borrowing costs for businesses that want to invest in buildings, property, machinery, equipment, and inventories. This is called "physical investment"—or simply "investment." Physical investment is distinguished from "financial investment," also called just "investment." The vocabulary of economists is sometimes strange and ambiguous, but in this case, the context usually makes clear whether physical or financial investment is under consideration.

The physical investment increases the country's "physical capital," meaning its total stock (quantity and quality) of factories, office buildings, machinery, equipment, and inventories. Also, with more capital to work with, workers become more productive. For both reasons, the production capacity of the country increases, and the economy grows faster.

There are problems with achieving growth in this way. First, it may be that most of the borrowing is by consumers to purchase homes and durable goods rather than by businesses to increase physical capital. Second, businesses may be pessimistic about future sales and therefore not borrow funds and consequently not expand physical capital. Third, banks may also be pessimistic, worried that their loans may not be paid back, and therefore refuse to lend. Fourth—the opposite danger—the economy might be in an expansion phase, and the lower interest rate would cause inflation rather than add to physical capital.

There are better ways to stimulate economic growth. In large part, growth depends on the quality of the workforce. Education and training should be fostered by government policies. Providing good health care for the population and promoting a healthful lifestyle are also ingredients. Improvements in technology—new commodities, improvements in the quality of existing commodities, and better and cheaper ways of producing commodities—are very important to assure economic growth. A free-enterprise system, whereby inventors and innovators (called "entrepreneurs") keep the profits on their accomplishments, provides incentives for entrepreneurs to develop and use improvements in technology.

The infrastructure should not be forgotten. One of the crucial functions of governments is to maintain and improve the economic infrastructure. That means both physical things (roads, bridges, airports, harbors, sewer systems) and human things (education and public health, as stated above). Without a sound economic infrastructure, growth policies will not work.

Finally, it should be emphasized that growth can have a negative feature. There is a price to be paid when an economy switches resources from producing for the present (consumer goods and services) to producing for the future (infrastructure and physical capital). Unless there is substantial unemployment, both consumer commodities and physical capital cannot be increased at the same time. In the short run at least, there is a sacrifice of consumption so that there can be more investment. The most serious examples of this are the old Soviet Union and former Communist China. By direct control, the governments of these countries starved consumption (in fact, sometimes literally starving people to death) in order to shift resources from producing consumer goods and services to producing physical capital.

This is not to say that growth is harmful. Rather, there is something to be said for the market determining the pace of economic growth. The government's role is to maintain and improve the physical and human infrastructure. If people want to provide for their future retirement, they will save more now. This means more funds are supplied to financial markets, which lowers interest rates. The lower interest rates stimulate business investment. As a consequence, the economy grows faster, and in the future produces the additional consumer goods and services that retirees want. That is the logic in having the interest rates *for growth* determined by the market rather than by the government, which might set interest rates too high or too low.

This argument leaves room for the central bank to determine interest rates from the standpoint of fighting recessions and inflation, reducing rates in recession and increasing them in inflation. But that would take place only for relatively short periods of time.

Q Can the United States continue to grow? And at what point is growth unsustainable?

A Let's begin by defining growth. Growth is the trend increase in per-capita real GDP (gross domestic product adjusted for inflation). This is the economy's inflation-corrected total output per person. Note that the GDP must be corrected for inflation; otherwise the growth is not physical, just nominal GDP or money GDP. For example, if money GDP goes up by 5 percent, but inflation is 3 percent, then real GDP increases by about 2 percent.

The real GDP concept used for growth is per capita, but for cycles it is real GDP itself. The economy's business cycle, which involves recessions and expansions, is measured according to the movement of real GDP around trend real GDP. The economy's growth is measured via the trend of *per capita* real GDP (GDP per inhabitant). Note that GDP for growth (per-capita [real] GDP) is not GDP per worker; rather it is GDP per inhabitant, whether or not the inhabitant is working.

Now your question can be answered. *Yes* to the first part; the United States can, and most probably will, continue to grow. There will still be the business cycle, but the *trend* in per-capita [real] GDP most likely will be upward, as it has been for many years.

Uncertain is the answer to the second part. In principle, many things can make growth unsustainable. The sources of growth (discussed below) can dry up; damage to the environment can be so great that it cannot be overcome; the demographic structure can involve an ever higher proportion of retired or other nonworking people; or there could be a natural catastrophe (a massive meteor landing on or near the Continental United States) or a human-made catastrophe (a nuclear war or widespread terrorism or civil strife). Most people believe that these unfavorable events will not happen to the United States during the foreseeable future, but we really don't know.

So let's return to examine the sources of U.S. growth, and consider government policies that would foster these sources and therefore help in sustaining U.S. growth. The workforce (labor) is crucial. Natural birth and immigration together assure an increasing population and therefore an increasing workforce. The danger here is that the demographic structure could shift in the direction of an aging, nonworking population. Sometimes changes in the culture act to increase the workforce. For example, the dramatic increase in married female workers tremendously expanded the labor force. Another source of increased labor supply would be more people opting for later retirement.

Physical capital—factories, office buildings, machinery, and equipment—that is directly used by firms in producing commodities grows via business investment in these items. Business investment is financed by domestic private savings and net capital inflow (foreigners investing in this country in greater amounts than we invest abroad). Increasing domestic private savings is paramount, because there is no guarantee that net capital flow will be inward to the United States indefinitely.

There is also human capital, meaning education, training, and good health embodied in labor. Expanding and improving education at all levels and universal medical care are public policies that would assure growth in human capital. For economic growth, one of the most important tasks of government is maintenance of the infrastructure, both physical (transportation and communication facilities—roads, bridges, canals, airports, cellular and broadcast frequencies, the Internet, and so on) and human (education and public health).

Technological improvement results in creation of new commodities, better quality of existing commodities, and cheaper ways of producing commodities. A good environment for invention (creation of something new) and innovation (installing that new thing in the production process) is critical. This means a legal system that protects intellectual property sufficient to encourage invention and innovation (via patent laws, for example) but not overly sufficient so that it takes too long for innovations to spread beyond patent holders.

Natural resources are an ingredient in economic growth. They are fixed in quantity but fortunately can be imported. In fact, international trade is a good growth policy, as it assures an efficient mix of the country's output (GDP): The country is exporting what it can produce more cheaply and more efficiently than other countries and importing what it could produce more expensively and less efficiently.

Efficiency in the production process increases productivity of all growth ingredients. Also, workers "learn by doing"—experience increases labor productivity.

In sum, there is reason for optimism. The United States continues to posses the ingredients for sustained economic growth. Sound growth-oriented government policy helps keep the growth process going.

Chapter 8

CENTRAL BANKS AND MONEY (THE FED)

Money, money, money. You can't buy happiness and true love with money, and you can't have a two-way conversation with money. But money can buy a lot of material things. Ever since money was invented—and that is many centuries ago—people have been fascinated with money. Questions about it abound, from what money really is to how the money supply is controlled. *Everyday Economics* does not evade these issues; it addresses them head-on in this chapter.

What is money?

We can say that, at least in the U.S. economy, money is "the dollar." But what does that mean?

Traditionally, economists see money as having three functions: unit of account, medium of exchange, and store of value. A *unit of account* is the unit in which prices are expressed, records of transactions are made, and valuations of assets and liabilities are kept. Without a common unit of account, records would be inconsistent and non-comparable. A *medium of exchange* is a facilitator of transactions. Without money as an intermediary, people and businesses would have to resort to barter, with all its inconveniences and inefficiencies. A *store of value* is an asset that permits transferring of purchasing power from one period to another—from present to future, in its simplest form.

While money is both the only unit of account and by far the most important medium of exchange, there are many other stores of value (for example, stocks, bonds, and real estate) and, in fact, money is not a particularly important store of value (mainly because money has a low expected return compared to other assets). Fortunately, in the modern economy, we do not have the complication of different moneys for the different functions of money. We are no longer in colonial times, when the unit of account was pounds, shillings, and pence (like the old English system), while the principal medium of exchange was the Spanish dollar (actually a coin, and forerunner of the U.S. dollar).

There are two general properties of money that are not unique to money. First, money is a stock rather than a flow. In other words, money exists at a point in time. Official statistics as well as economic writings refer to the "money stock" or "stock of money"; though often the term "money supply" is used. While *changes* in the money stock are flows, the *level* of the money stock is (as the term itself indicates) a stock. Second, money is an asset (meaning something owned) to the holder of money. It is also a corresponding liability (meaning something owed: a debt or obligation) to the issuer of money. The implication is that the money stock cannot be measured by including all holders and all issuers. That's because, if you cancel assets and liabilities, the result would be a zero money stock.

There are two official definitions of the U.S. money stock, termed M1 and M2. M1 is founded on a strict definition of money as a medium of exchange. In particular, M1 consists of public holdings of (1) currency, meaning coins and bills; (2) traveler's checks; and (3) checkable deposits at financial institutions such as banks, savings and loan associations, and credit unions. The "public" means individuals and nonfinancial institutions such as businesses and nonprofit organizations. For lack of separate data, the "public" includes foreigners in the case of currency. Issuers of M1 are the Treasury (for coin), the Federal Reserve (for currency), and financial institutions (for traveler's checks and checkable deposits). These entities are not considered part of the public, so their holdings of money are excluded from M1.

M2 adds some other stores of value to M1: savings deposits, time deposits (such as "certificates of deposit," or CDs) less than $100,000, money-market deposit accounts, and balances in retail money-market mutual funds. Obviously, many stores of value (such as stocks, bonds, and real estate) remain excluded from M2.

Checks and debit cards are not money. Rather, they are instruments that transfer money from one holder to another. Also, credit card balances are not money. They are loans that the credit card companies make to us. Of course, money is used to pay the credit card debt.

People often ask: "What gives money its value?" Economists ask themselves the same question. The answer often given by economists is: "general acceptability." But what gives money the property of "general acceptability"? At one time, paper currency and banks did not exist. Gold and silver, which are tangible commodities, constituted money. Cigarettes were money for Allied prisoners in German prisoner-of-war camps in World War II. It is easy to see that these "commodity monies" had at least part of their value based on their non-monetary usefulness.

Money today is currency and deposits, which economists call "fiat money," meaning something made money by decree of an authority.

Currency and deposits are money because the government in effect declares them to be money. So "general acceptability" is enhanced by the government. However, the "general acceptability" of money is in large part a circular phenomenon: we accept money because we are confident that other economic entities (people, financial institutions, other businesses, government) will accept that money. In other words, money is generally accepted because it is generally accepted! If that seems weird to you, you may be interested to know that it is also weird to many economists.

What is "liquidity"? And what does it mean for a market to be "liquid" or "not liquid"?

"Liquidity" of an asset refers to the speed, convenience, and cost of converting that asset to immediate purchasing power of goods, services, securities, and so on, or what is called "generalized purchasing power." The most liquid asset of all is money—currency and bank deposits upon which checks can be written—because money itself has generalized purchasing power. If you have money, you can spend it immediately on whatever is available for purchase, and you don't have to convert the money into what it already is (generalized purchasing power). Of course, we are assuming that the money you have to spend is genuine. The seller of whatever you buy is confident that the currency is not counterfeit and that the money in your deposit account is there to cover the amount of the check you write.

Other assets are less liquid. They have to be converted into money before they can be spent. Further, this conversion can involve your time, expense, and risk. If you have a certificate of deposit (CD) in a bank and you cash it in prior to maturity, you have to pay a penalty, including loss of interest. If you have a bond (even a government bond) and sell it prior to maturity (you could sell it in the market, but not back to the issuer), then there is the risk that your selling price of the bond is lower than the price at which you bought the bond. Of course, the risk could be to your benefit: the selling price of the bond *might* be higher than the buying price.

If you own stock and want to convert some of it to money, the situation is even more uncertain. Stocks, unlike CDs and bonds, have no maturity date. As long as the issuing company remains in existence, the stock goes on as well. So no matter when you sell the stock you either could make a profit (selling at higher than the purchase price) or take a loss (selling at lower than the purchase price).

In addition, there is a commission you pay to a broker for carrying out the transaction. Instead of (or even in addition to) the commission, there is a "bid–ask spread." No matter what the "market price" of the bond or stock, you have to pay a somewhat higher price to buy it and can sell only at a somewhat lower price. Also, you have to wait until the transaction is completed before you receive your money.

The situation is even worse for physical assets. If you want to sell your car or house, then the price is even more uncertain than for a bond or stock, and furthermore the price is dependent on bargaining, with all its hassles. Further, for something like a house, there could be a substantial delay from the time you decide to sell to the time that you receive the money.

Why hold these less-liquid or "illiquid" (not at all liquid) assets at all? The reason is that they can give you a high return (interest, dividends, or profits)—much higher than the return on money, which for currency is zero and for checkable deposits is low compared to the expected return on bonds, stocks, and real estate. Of course, the return on these less-liquid assets is not a sure thing; that is why it is only an "expected" return. You could even suffer a loss when you sell the asset. That loss is impossible with money, but the expected return on money is less than on less-liquid assets.

What about liquidity of an entire market for an asset or group of assets? Here liquidity means that the market can experience a large amount of transactions with only a slight effect on the market price. In contrast, an "illiquid market" (also called a "thin market") suffers large changes in price for a small amount of transactions. One virtue of the stock and bond markets that governments like and that financial institutions brag about is that the typical investor can buy or sell a substantial amount of a particular stock or bond without "moving the market" (changing the market price). In other words, the market is liquid.

By the way, a liquid market is *not* also called a "thick market," even though an "illiquid market" is termed a "thin market." Don't ask me why there is no vocabulary symmetry, because I don't know.

Q What is monetary policy and how does it work?

A Monetary policy is the use of instruments by the central bank to control the money supply (the money stock), which consists of currency and bank deposits held by the public. The "public" excludes the banking system, meaning not only banks but all financial institutions that have deposit liabilities. The money supply is controlled not directly but only indirectly. The banking system has reserves, consisting of currency in its vaults (*not* part of the money supply) and its deposits with the central bank. These reserves are assets of the banks; they are the source of cash to honor requests by depositors to withdraw their deposits in whole or part. Note that deposits are assets of the deposit holders, but liabilities of the bank.

A fundamental fact is that banks hold reserves that account for only a fraction of their deposit liabilities. That is important for their profits, because the loans made and securities bought are income-earning assets (the counterpart of deposits), whereas reserves earn no interest. Early in their history, banks discovered that only part of their deposits would be cashed in (or lost via check-clearing with other banks); therefore it made sense to hold reserves in smaller amounts than deposit liabilities.

Central banks refine the banking practice by having minimum reserve requirements as a percentage of deposit liabilities of banks. This percentage (which can be zero) can vary with the type, size, and location of the financial institution, as well as the type and amount of the deposit. Therefore deposits of the banking system are a multiple of its reserves.

One way for the central bank to increase (or decrease) the money supply is by reducing (or increasing) reserve requirements. Another way is by lending to banks, thus increasing the banking system's deposits at the central bank and potentially increasing the money supply (if the banks lend more to individuals and businesses). By worsening the lending terms (increasing the interest rate charged to banks) or even rationing borrowing (refusing to lend to banks), the central bank can decrease the money supply.

The third way of affecting the money supply is the usual instrument of choice: open-market operations. The central bank buys securities either from the banks themselves or from the banks' customers. It pays for the securities by increasing the banks' deposits at the central bank. This happens directly if the purchases are from banks, indirectly if the purchases are from the public. In the latter case, the central bank writes a check on itself, which the recipient deposits in her or its financial institution, which then sends the check to the central bank and receives a corresponding increase in its deposits at the central bank. Either way, banking-system reserves go up, permitting increases in bank lending and in the money supply. Of course, if the central bank sells securities, then everything goes into reverse and the money supply is reduced.

There are many issues in monetary policy. Three are mentioned here. The first issue is how monetary policy works to increase the economy's output (in a recession) or to reduce inflationary pressure (in an overexpansion of the economy). Many economists think that increasing the money supply or its rate of growth reduces interest rates, which stimulates borrowing, and therefore spending, by individuals and businesses. The same line or reasoning applies in reverse to a reduction in the money supply. Some economists, called "monetarists," have a different view. They believe that the increased money *directly* increases spending, because it "burns a hole in the pocket" if it is not spent; so no decrease in the interest rate is necessary. Similarly, less money means there is less spending, again directly and not through interest rates.

The second issue is whether the central bank should have a target growth rate for the money supply or a target interest rate for the economy. Monetarists advocate the former, but central banks have opted for the latter. For example, the Federal Reserve (the U.S. central bank) has a target federal-funds rate. The federal-funds rate is the interest rate at which banks lend and borrow deposits that they have at the Fed to and from each other. As the federal-funds rate goes, so do the other interest rates in the economy.

A third issue is that the central bank, through its three instruments, can force the banking system to contract its deposits, thus reducing the money supply or its rate of growth. But it cannot force the banking system to expand its deposits; so the money supply or its rate of growth does not necessarily increase. It is easier for the central bank to fight inflation than recession! Why would banks not want to expand their deposits, even with more reserves? Because they could be scared that loans would not be paid back. A recession could be caused by pessimism about the future of the economy, and could itself generate pessimism about the future of the economy.

◻ What does the Fed Chair do? How does that differ from the Treasury Chair?

◻ The formal names are "Chairman of the Board of Governors of the Federal Reserve System" (abbreviated as the "Fed chairman" or "Fed chair") and "Secretary of the Treasury" (abbreviated as "Treasury secretary"). First, consider how they get their positions. Both are appointed by the president and confirmed by the Senate. The Fed chairman must first be appointed a member of the Board of Governors of the Federal Reserve System (there are seven such members), and also must be confirmed. So the Fed chairman experiences two appointments and two Senate confirmations. Appointment to the Board of Governors is for a nonrenewable 14-year term; appointment as Chair is for a renewable 4-year term.

The Treasury Secretary serves at the pleasure of the president, and can be dismissed at any time. In contrast, the president cannot do that to the Fed chair. The Federal Reserve in general, and the Fed chair in particular, is essentially independent of the president, apart from the appointment procedure. Ultimately, the Federal Reserve owes its accountability only to Congress, which at any time can amend the legislation under which the Federal Reserve operates.

It is fair to say that the Fed chair has a greater influence on the economy than does the Treasury secretary and has the more prestigious job. In fact, the Fed chairman is sometimes described as the second most powerful person in the United States! No one would say that about the Treasury secretary, who is only fifth in line in the presidential succession order. It is true that the Fed chair is not a Cabinet member and not in the presidential succession line; but no matter, that does not affect his or her influence and prestige.

What do they do? The Fed chair heads the Federal Reserve, which is responsible for the monetary policy of the country. It does this primarily via open-market operations, buying and selling *existing* government bonds. Suppose the Fed buys bonds. It does this by writing checks to the sellers of the bonds, who deposit the checks in their banks. The banks present the checks to the Fed, which increases the deposits of the banks at the Fed. These deposits are reserves of the banking system. (The process is simpler, if the Fed buys bonds from the banks themselves. Then the Fed pays directly by increasing the banks' deposits at the Fed.) So bank reserves increase, and the banks proceed to expand their lending, creating deposits in the process. The opposite is true for the Fed selling securities. So open-market operations change the rate of growth of the money supply. The Fed also supervises and regulates banks, making sure that the financial system is secure and protecting credit rights of consumers.

The Treasury secretary heads the Department of the Treasury, which is in charge of the finances of the federal government, especially the collection of taxes and paying bills. It also manages the public debt of the government. The Treasury secretary advises the president on economic policy, but is not the only advisor. The Treasury issues (creates) government bonds and sells them in the marketplace, usually to private parties. Note that the Fed does not issue bonds; it deals only in existing bonds.

How does the Fed differ from other, overseas monetary institutions?

Perhaps the most important difference is that, compared to almost all other central banks, the Fed has greater independence in monetary policy. And monetary policy is the most important task of a central bank.

Economists identify two aspects of central-bank independence: independence in setting goals (the objectives of monetary policy) and independence in the policy operations used to carry out goals. Independence means independent of the government, the political authority. In practice, the government is represented by the Treasury or Department of Finance.

The Fed is independent of the U.S. Treasury in both aspects. The Swiss National Bank is thought to have even greater independence than the Fed. The European Central Bank (ECB) essentially has independence comparable to the Fed. While treaty establishes price stability (absence of inflation, or, in practice, low inflation) as the primary goal of the ECB, it is free to interpret that goal. In spite of its long history compared to other central banks, the Bank of England is independent only in the policies used to carry out goals; its policy goal (a precise inflation target) is set by the British Treasury.

Central banks with low independence are those of some developing countries and/or of countries with authoritarian governments. It is unlikely that the People's Bank of China would disobey instructions from the Chinese government. The danger of lack of independence in these countries (but not in China) is that the government orders the central bank to purchase government debt in large amounts and inconsistent with the goal of low inflation. In some countries and sometimes the central bank literally "prints money" (prints currency) in phenomenal amounts, in order to finance government spending. Needless to say, the consequences for inflation and for confidence in the country's currency can be serious indeed. Because the Chinese government traditionally insists that the People's Bank of China have a conservative monetary policy, these events are not likely to happen in that country.

The Fed, and the central banks of other large developed countries, has the advantage of a large capital market, which facilitates the policy instrument of "open-market operations." That means purchases and sales of domestic government bonds to alter the reserves of the banking sector and therefore change the rate of growth of the money supply. In countries without such a market, monetary policy is more difficult. Open-market operations are the most precise kind of monetary policy; they can be calibrated to a precise degree.

All is not lost for countries lacking a substantial capital market. Central banks buying (selling) *anything* increases (decreases) reserves of the banking system. The thing doesn't have to be domestic-government bonds. In particular, the central bank can buy and sell foreign exchange (for example, the dollar or euro) instead of bonds. But then the exchange rate may be affected in a way that the country and its central bank do not want. The central bank buying foreign exchange pushes up the price of the foreign currency in terms of domestic currency. In other words, it pushes down the price of the domestic currency in terms of foreign currency. The central bank selling foreign exchange has the opposite effect. The central bank might not like the resulting change in the exchange rate. Then there is a conflict between monetary policy's domestic effect (change the money supply in the desired direction) and foreign effect (change the exchange rate in an undesired direction).

Chapter 9

ECONOMIC SYSTEMS (CAPITALISM AND COMMUNISM)

At one time there was a lot of controversy among economists, political scientists, and the general public as to whether capitalism or communism would prevail in the world. Guess what? Capitalism won. The communist countries have become a lot more like us than we have become like them. And capitalism carries with it the market system, whereby economic decisions are made by individuals and businesses acting in their own interests and guided by market prices. Issues about capitalism both in and of itself and versus communism or socialism remain. In this chapter, *Everyday Economics* answers some provocative questions of that nature.

◎ What would happen if the middle class disappears?

🅰 If the middle class disappears, there would be profound social, political, and economic consequences. The middle class has cultural and ethical values that set the social tone in modern countries. The "work ethic," volunteer work for charities (as distinct from large individual contributions), and affinity to neighborhoods are among the values associated with the middle class. Of course, some poor people and some rich people also have these values. So whether these values would entirely disappear without a middle class is uncertain; but it is indisputable that the existence of a large middle class in the population fosters these values.

Politically, the middle class is associated with democracy. When the population consisted of largely the extreme rich (nobility) and the extreme poor (peasants and serfs) with a very small middle class, democracy did not take hold. Whether the growth of a middle class in China carries with it democracy to replace an authoritarian government remains to be seen—but history is on the side of democracy uplifted by a rising middle class.

Economically, the "middle class" is defined as the group of people who are neither rich nor poor. Scholars can argue as to which measure of the middle class is best. To put it another way, there is no agreement on how high your income or wealth has to be to classify you as rich, nor on how low to classify you as poor. But almost everyone knows where he or she would be classified according to any reasonable definition.

If the middle class disappears, an array of industries oriented to goods and services consumed by the middle class would shrink drastically—from public universities to serviceable yet stylistic clothing, from personal computers to moderate-cost single-family housing. Production in these and any other industries that remain would have great difficulty finding trained workers who do "middle-class jobs." An economy consisting of only the rich and the poor would probably revert to a sharply reduced total output (real GDP, or gross domestic product in "real terms," correcting for inflation or deflation). Per-capita real GDP would also fall, although the concept would have little meaning in an economy consisting of only rich (high per-capita real income) and poor (low per-capita real income).

The disappearance of the middle class is an extremely unlikely event. During major wars, there was concern that military occupations susceptible to high casualty rates were composed mainly of the middle class, which could substantially reduce the middle-class population. Some fear today that the middle class could vanish through tax policy, that is, the government overly taxing middle-income brackets, while the poor receive subsidies (welfare) instead of paying taxes and the rich have substantial tax breaks to compensate for high tax rates. The highly educated and hardest-working component of the middle class would shift to the rich group; the less-educated and less-motivated component to the poor.

In my view, the middle class is here to stay for at least several more generations. Nevertheless, there is understandable frustration of middle-class people with government policies that are overly oriented to the poor and to the rich segments of the population. The middle class generally feels neglected or abandoned—except during political campaigns, when politicians vie with one another to show they have the interests of the middle class foremost in their minds and policies.

Q What is nationalization, and how does it affect economic growth?

A Nationalization means firms owned by government rather than private individuals, partnerships, or corporations. Strictly speaking, nationalization is the *act* of changing ownership of firms from the private sector to the government. But the question is logically interpreted as pertaining to firms already nationalized. The ultimate in nationalization (or, more precisely, nationalized industry) is socialism, under which the government owns all, or nearly all, firms in the economy. The question then becomes: Is government ownership of industry good for economic growth?

Some economists think that, *under ideal conditions*, government ownership would be better for economic growth than private ownership. They believe that, in each industry, the government could behave as a benevolent monopolist, and could establish the pricing and production policies that would bring about the most economic efficiency. A privately owned monopoly would not do this, because it would be detrimental to the monopolist's own profits. The problem is that ideal conditions do not apply. The government may claim that it runs nationalized industry with the objective of economic efficiency, but it most probably lacks the information and the capacity to carry it out.

A nationalized industry lacks the profit motivation that makes firms foster efficiency. This is clear when the alternative to government ownership is many firms (true competition) in the industry. But even when the alternative is only a single firm (private monopoly), at least the monopolist enhances its profits by always producing any given amount at lowest cost. There is no profit incentive for a government monopoly. Any profits go to the state, the overall government. Also, the manager, even the CEO equivalent (whatever the head manager is called under nationalization), has incentive only to keep his job and not make waves by engaging in entrepreneurial activity. Creation of new products and creation of cheaper ways of producing existing products will be slower than under private ownership.

It is true that the old-time Soviet economy, when it was the Soviet Union and embraced socialism, at times experienced rapid economic growth. But that growth was concentrated in heavy industry, including the military. It was not the type of growth that the bulk of the population wanted. In fact, consumers had their standard of living reduced, and, under extreme circumstance, were literally starved, so that the economy (especially heavy and military industries) could grow.

What went along with socialism was a command economy. Instead of the free-market price system, there were government-controlled prices and government orders to firms on what and how much to produce. The economic inefficiency of socialism and a command economy became apparent in the transition of the Soviet, Eastern European, and Chinese economies from socialism and command economies to capitalism (private ownership of industry) and the free-market price system. Under the free-market price system (our system), market prices guide the decisions of consumers and businesses.

There are some nationalized industries in the United States, such as the U.S. Post Office (for delivery to mailboxes) and Amtrak (for passenger intercity train service). Neither is a model of economic efficiency. In addition to the absence of the private profit incentive, there is the political element of the government providing above-market wages and benefits that would not be acceptable to a privately owned firm. The government is typically weaker in labor negotiations than is private industry, although there are occasionally exceptions due to special circumstances. Air traffic controllers are the best example of a tough U.S. government attitude toward the workforce, which began under President Reagan.

The opposite of nationalization is privatization; the conversion of government ownership to private ownership. Then the advantages of private ownership for economic efficiency and economic growth could be realized, although it could take time.

Q In what big ways does the American economy differ from the economies of other wealthy Western nations, such as Canada, the UK, France, and Germany?

A The similarities between the United States and the four countries mentioned are much more important than the differences. All five countries are developed industrial countries and have high per-capita income (expressing their GDP in a common currency, such as U.S. dollars, and dividing by population) and are market economies. Politically, the countries are true democracies, with governments that are not authoritarian. They are allies, all members of NATO.

There are some meaningful differences among the countries, though not in the sense of the United States versus the other four. Germany, France, and the UK are members of the European Union (EU). They have free trade in goods and services, and also free movement of people and capital—not only among themselves but also among the other members of the EU. Further, the EU has a common trade policy (tariffs and other trade restrictions) versus the rest of the world, including Canada and the United States. Naturally, free immigration within the EU does not extend to people outside that organization.

The United States and Canada, along with Mexico, are members of the North American Free Trade Agreement (NAFTA). The three countries have free movement of goods and services among themselves—but decidedly *not* free immigration. Thus there remains the issue of illegal (undocumented) Mexican workers in the United States. Unlike the EU members, the United States, Canada, and Mexico have their own trade policies versus the rest of the world.

France and Germany are euro countries. Their national currencies are defunct, as are their national monetary policies. The European Central Bank is responsible for monetary policy for the entire euro area. In contrast, the United States, Canada, and the United Kingdom retain their own currencies and their own monetary policy.

One important difference between the United States and the other four countries as a group is the extent to which the "welfare state" has been adopted. Canada, the United Kingdom, France and Germany have a broader "safety net" for people in terms of health care, housing, welfare in general, old-age pensions, and so on. Whether that is good or bad for economic efficiency and growth is a matter of debate. A strong welfare state enhances the physical and mental well-being of workers, presumably making them more productive. However, a strong welfare state removes some work incentive, because the basic needs of people are covered in any event. It also tends to have high tax rates, again discouraging work incentives.

Q What is the biggest difference between a capitalist versus a socialist versus a communist economy?

A The biggest difference is the issue of who owns businesses and especially physical capital (factories, machinery, equipment). Under capitalism, persons own the businesses and physical capital. These persons can be individuals, partners, or corporations (legally persons, though owned by many individuals—the stockholders). Under socialism, the state owns the businesses and physical capital. According to Marxist theory, under pure communism (which has never existed in any country), there is no state; so the entity or entities that would own businesses and physical capital is unclear. Sometimes the words "socialism" and "communism" are used interchangeably.

Of course, all economies are mixes of capitalism and socialism, although there are different mixes for different countries. The United States is probably the industrial country with the heaviest capitalist component. Without a doubt, the transition of extreme socialist countries—the ex-Soviet Union (divided into multiple countries), Eastern European countries under Soviet influence, and China—from socialism to capitalism is a fascinating economic event.

Normally, capitalism is associated with a market economy and socialism with a command economy. In a market economy, economic activity (production, consumption, and trade) is coordinated by the actions of individual decision makers acting in accordance with price signals. In a command economy, economic activity is coordinated by central planning and decree. Again, all economies are a mix of the market and government intervention, with different mixes for different countries. It is only logical that the same countries that move from socialism to capitalism also move from a command economy to the free market.

Q Isn't an advantage of communism over capitalism that communism has a job for everyone? Is "consumer sovereignty" an advantage of capitalism?

A When the "communist" economies of China, the old Soviet Union, and Eastern Europe were in existence, they did provide jobs for almost everyone. Typically people did not have complete freedom of travel, so they could not change location to get new jobs. Also, with a "command economy," the opportunity for entrepreneurship and wealth accumulation was limited. The economy was government-run and heavy-industry oriented. The consumer was considered last. The quantity, quality, and variety of consumer goods and services available were much more limited than in Western capitalist, market economies. The incentive to work hard was not there, both because people were already provided with jobs and because they could not buy much with their earnings. A widespread saying among workers in communist countries was: "They pretend to pay us, and we pretend to work."

A capitalist market economy has "consumer sovereignty." This means that commodities are produced in accordance with the demands of consumers and not via instructions of a dictator or central planning board. Consumer sovereignty is not necessarily fair. You may think that your desires for commodities give you a "vote" on what and how much of consumer goods and services are to be produced. But that vote "counts" *only if* it carries with it the ability and willingness to pay for the goods and services. It is "one dollar, one vote" rather than "one person, one vote." A rich person's influence in the markets for consumer goods and services counts much more than a poor person's influence. You can reasonably judge that situation to be "unfair."

Consumer sovereignty can also be viewed as leading to immoral outcomes. Consider some types of commodities that are produced in capitalist market economies: pornographic literature and films, designer clothing, pet rocks, virtual pets, electronic games with violent orientation. Some observers judge that array of goods as immoral, and would prefer that it be replaced with more production of religious literature, modest clothing, and nonviolent electronic games. Again that view cannot be contradicted on moral grounds.

However, one could ask who better than the consumer to make decisions on what goods and services to consume? If some consumers have greater wealth, they have a greater say in these decisions. We can argue about income redistribution from rich to poor, but that is a separate matter from consumer sovereignty. As far as judgments on types of commodities produced are concerned, inevitably certain commodities will be considered inappropriate or immoral by some individuals. These people need not purchase the commodities and also can try to educate others to avoid the commodities. If their arguments work, then consumers in general will cut back on their demand for these commodities and there will be less production of them.

Q Could national economies reach a right balance between government economic intervention and market freedom?

A In principle, yes. From the standpoint of economic efficiency, the government should intervene in the economy only under certain conditions. First, the government should provide "public goods," such as national defense, police and fire protection, snow removal, and public health. You can't rely on private business to produce these items, because they could not prevent nonpurchasers from enjoying these "goods" and therefore no one would voluntarily pay for them.

Second, the government should intervene in economic activities with side effects: It should tax activities that generate bad consequences for those not carrying out the activity, such as chemical production that causes pollution, and it should subsidize activities that have good consequences for those not carrying out the activity, such as basic scientific research. Third, the government should provide infrastructure (roads, bridges, education). Fourth, there needs to be a legal system to make laws and adjudicate disputes.

Unfortunately, reality intrudes. Unless one carries out sophisticated polling of people (which is not done), it is impossible to determine efficiently how much of each "public good" to produce. In addition to "public goods," the government also produces "private goods," which are better left entirely to private business. The U.S. Post Office is a good example. Activities with side effects can be taxed or subsidized, but it is often hard to measure the actual amount of the good or bad side effect and to determine the appropriate tax rate or subsidy rate. Infrastructure and the legal system appear clear-cut, but that is not the case. There can easily be too little or too much expenditure on infrastructure, and the legal system is full of problems, partly because laws can have good intentions but undesirable side effects.

Yes, the market can "fail" to do its job correctly, but so too can the government when it tries to correct the market. So, in practice, it is unlikely that the right balance between government intervention and market freedom can be achieved.

Another complication is that much government intervention is for the purpose of subsidizing people or organizations (especially businesses) without the motivation of enhancing economic efficiency. Some subsidies redistribute income from richer to poorer people; other subsidies redistribute income from taxpayers to corporations. These acts of government are political facts of life, but they detract from economic efficiency. Unfortunately, our very democratic system of government provides the opportunity for government actions that detract from economic efficiency.

Chapter 10

GLOBALIZATION (GLOBAL ECONOMY AND YOU)

The power of economics is seen at all levels—from the decisions of an individual person to the workings of the global economy. In the final chapter, *Everyday Economics* provides insight into the globalization issues that people wonder and worry about. And the final question asks what could happen should globalization end.

Q Define free trade. Is it really free?

A "Free trade" means international transactions in goods and services that take place strictly according to market considerations. There are no tariffs, which are taxes on imports but not on domestic production of the same or similar commodities. There are no other government interferences with trade, such as quotas that set limits on the quantity of commodities that can be imported. Even so, trade would not really be free in the sense that it is truly unencumbered, for the following reasons.

1. *There are frictions in international trade that are not imposed by government:* in particular, transportation costs and transactions costs. It is usually true that these costs are greater in international rather than domestic trade, because of the elements of greater distance, different legal systems, and different cultures. But there are exceptions. For example, trade between Michigan and Ontario could easily involve lower costs than trade between Maine and Texas.

2. *Even if there are zero tariffs and zero other trade barriers among a group of countries, in a real sense this trade is not free.* Consider the European Union (EU). By removing trade barriers among themselves but retaining trade barriers against outside countries, each EU country gives a competitive advantage to other EU industries, as compared to industries in outside countries. So, for example, France may import a commodity from Italy even though the United States could provide the commodity at a lower price. The reason is that the U.S. exporter is faced with a tariff or other trade barrier to overcome, while the Italian exporter has no such obstacle.

3. *Even if trade is legally free, governments may interfere in other ways with the free movement of goods and services between countries.* For example, imports may be discouraged by administrative regulations that favor domestic producers. An example is safety and environmental rules that could be

established to make it easy for domestic firms to obey and hard for foreign firms to meet. Sometimes it is not clear whether a safety regulation, put in place allegedly to keep dangerous products from being marketed, is truly for safety or really just to keep out imports.

4. *Intellectual property rights may not be respected internationally.* The U.S. government and U.S. corporations have a history of complaining that patents and trademarks of U.S. firms are not respected in some other countries, such as India and China. For example, Indian firms produce versions of drugs still under patent owned by U.S. pharmaceutical companies, while Chinese firms copy Hollywood films and books copywritten by publishers in the United States and other countries. They often do this without permission of the patent or copyright holder. Trademarks are also violated. A U.S. brand name may be attached to a product manufactured in India or China by firms that have no relationship to the U.S. company. These shenanigans could occur quite in accordance with foreign law, or even perhaps against the law but with the passive acquiescence of the foreign government. Certainly, there are less U.S. exports because of such violations of intellectual property rights.

5. *Free trade does not encompass government over-encouraging trade.* Too much trade is no more consistent with the free market than is too little trade. Government subsidies to commodity exporters—even if the subsidies are not directly tied to exports—are just as much interferences with free trade as are tariffs. Agricultural products and aircraft are two commodity classes for which subsidies are prevalent.

In fact, except for regional organizations such as the EU, trade is still subject to tariff and nontariff barriers (especially quotas limiting the amount of foreign goods that can be imported). True, these barriers have been reduced over time and even removed for some classes of commodities—but they are still there. Economists and government officials are aware that textiles and agricultural products are two classes of commodities that are far from enjoying free trade.

◩ What do imports and exports really mean, and how do the statistics we hear about them affect individual economies?

◪ The U.S. balance of payments is a record of all economic transactions between residents of the United States and residents of other countries. "Residents" includes individuals, households, businesses, and governments (local, state, and federal). The balance of payments is kept quarterly, except that the goods-and-services account is available monthly.

Every month the government provides data on exports of goods and services, imports of goods and services, and the deficit in goods and services. The exports (or imports) figure is the dollar value of all goods and services that U.S. residents sell to (or buy from) the rest of the world. The balance on goods and services is the exports figure minus the imports figure, and is also called net exports of goods and services, or net receipts from goods and services. This *goods-and-services account* is in surplus or deficit, according to whether exports are greater or less than imports of goods and services.

Exports of goods and services are desirable because they involve a demand for, and therefore increase, the country's output and employment (to produce the output). Imports of goods and services are beneficial because they enhance the country's standard of living (more goods and services to consume and invest). The balance in goods and services is important in the sense that a surplus adds to, and a deficit subtracts from, U.S. total output of goods and services (the GDP, or gross domestic product). In that sense it can be argued that a surplus increases, and a deficit reduces, U.S. employment.

However, more important than the balance on goods and services is the fact that, in exporting goods and services that we produce cheaper than abroad, and in importing goods and services produced cheaper abroad, both countries gain. In particular, U.S. residents gain. We gain in overall productivity of our workers and in economic efficiency.

Other items in the balance of payments are available only quarterly. The *income account* has two main components: investment income and compensation of employees. Investment income receipts are composed of interest and dividends earned by U.S. residents on assets (stocks, bonds, businesses, and bank accounts) abroad. Employee compensation receipts include wages, salaries, and benefits earned by U.S. residents working in other countries. Payments on income accounts go in the opposite direction. Net income receipts are receipts minus payments.

Net *unilateral transfers* are the amount of gifts received by U.S. residents from residents of other countries minus the amount of gifts donated by U.S. residents to foreign residents.

Now add the balance in goods and services, net income receipts, and net unilateral transfers. This overall balance is called the *balance on current account.* Note the composition of this balance: it is receipts minus payments emanating from flows of goods and services, investment income, worker income, and gifts. The current-account balance has great importance. Suppose the United States is in current-account deficit. From that fact, we can say that the United States is living beyond its means. Our current (meaning expected, regular) payments to foreigners exceed our current (expected, regular) receipts from foreigners. We are paying more in dollars than we receive in dollars. Therefore foreign businesses, households, governments, and central banks end up with an increase in their dollar holdings.

What do the foreigners do with their increased dollars? They invest them in the United States. So, in net terms (because there is typically also some increase in U.S. investment abroad), our debt to foreigners has increased. Foreigners now own more stocks, bonds, businesses, and bank accounts in the United States. Is that a problem? There is at least one advantage. The net foreign investment in this country means an increased flow of funds into our financial institutions, which lowers interest rates, resulting in improved lending terms (lower interest rates) for borrowers.

However, the consequence of continuing to live beyond our means is that foreigners own more and more assets located in the United States. Our investment balance will continue to worsen, as our interest and dividend payments to foreigners increase, due to their increased holdings of U.S. income-paying assets. Can the foreign investment go on for a long time? Possibly, if foreigners actually want to hold ever more assets in this country. But eventually the foreigners may feel overloaded with dollar assets, sell the assets, and take their funds elsewhere. That could disrupt U.S. financial markets by greatly depressing prices of stocks and bonds and increasing interest rates tremendously.

There is also an issue of national sovereignty. To the extent that the increased foreign investment in this country takes the form of ownership of companies, foreigners increase their direct control of U.S. production. That may not be a problem if the foreign owners behave no differently than U.S. owners would. But what if the foreign owners take orders from their governments who happen not to be U.S. allies? It is this fear that keeps the U.S. government from approving foreign investment in certain crucial sectors of the economy.

Q Isn't the shift of manufacturing from the United States to China and India due to "unfair trade"? After all, U.S. manufacturing technology is just as good as in these countries, but foreign companies don't pay U.S. taxes or U.S. wages.

A The shift in a country's focus of production from basic manufacturing to high-tech manufacturing to services continues a progression that began with the shift from agriculture to basic manufacturing. Developed countries such as the United States go through these changes. The basic, and even high-tech, manufacturing moves somewhere, and the growing economies of China and India are the natural locations. One can predict that eventually China and India will lose their manufacturing to other developing countries. That process may have already begun.

That said, there has to be a logical economic reason for the U.S. loss and Chinese or Indian gain of manufacturing industries. It is true that U.S. wages are high compared to Chinese or Indian wages (converted to U.S. dollars)—but that is true as an economy-wide average. *All* U.S. companies, not just in the U.S. manufacturing industry, pay U.S. wages and U.S. taxes. Yet many U.S. companies successfully compete with foreign companies, and even export commodities to China and India. How can that be? The answer is that the productivity of U.S. workers (largely due to more physical capital, and superior technology) is higher than the productivity of workers abroad. Suppose that U.S. wages are generally three times as high as in China and India. Thus, any industry in which U.S. worker productivity is more than three times as high as in China or India is a good candidate to thrive domestically and export (even to China and India).

Then why is the United States in deficit on goods and services, importing a higher dollar amount of goods and services than exporting? One reason is that foreign countries and foreign residents *want* to invest their financial capital (buy more assets) in the United States more than American residents want to invest abroad. To compensate, U.S. residents buy more foreign goods and services than foreigners buy U.S. goods and services.

Another reason that the United States imports more than it exports revolves around the exchange rate. Consider the case of China. The Chinese central bank keeps the yuan at an artificially low value compared to the U.S. dollar. Suppose the actual exchange rate is 8 yuan per dollar, whereas the true-equilibrium market exchange rate would be 6 yuan per dollar. Then it takes 25 percent less dollars to buy a yuan, or 33 percent more yuan to buy a dollar, than under a free-market exchange rate. This discrepancy makes Chinese commodities much cheaper to U.S. residents than they would be under the free-market exchange rate. Also, U.S. commodities are much more expensive to Chinese residents. This situation increases the dollar amount of U.S. imports of goods and services and reduces the dollar amount of U.S. exports of goods and services.

If the yuan/dollar exchange rate were close to the free-market rate, then *some* U.S. manufacturing industry would be restored and *some* existing manufacturing industry would expand. Obviously, the U.S. government puts periodic pressure on the Chinese to free the yuan/dollar exchange rate either completely or partially, so that it reaches or comes closer to the free-market rate. That would make the yuan stronger (at the extreme, only 6, instead of 8, yuan per dollar). The Chinese government is reluctant to comply, because it likes the idea of exporting a lot more than it imports. To placate the United States—that is, for good political relationships—China does allow the yuan to get slightly stronger from time to time.

Q I understand that the United States restricts imports of sugar. Is that a good or bad policy?

A Sometimes the government adopts economic policies with the intention of helping only a small group in the economy. An example is restrictions on the imports of certain commodities. The tariff (tax) and quota (import limitation) system on imports of sugar is set up purely to keep the U.S. sugar-producing industry operating at a high profit level. Sugar is produced in the United States, but very inefficiently (that is, at a high cost) compared to production elsewhere in the world.

Who gains from U.S. sugar policy? The domestic sugar producers, who get a higher price for their product. Who loses? Two groups: the industries (candy, soft beverages, ice cream, and so on) that use sweeteners, and consumers. Why do consumers lose? They either pay more for these candy and beverages, or they pay the same price for an inferior product. The product is inferior because the industries use more corn sweetener (which is now less expensive compared to sugar) and less sugar. If you don't think that makes a difference, take the ice-cream taste test. Try ice cream with corn sweetener and then ice cream with sugar. As for "chocolate" made with corn sweetener instead of sugar—I, for one, would not try that product even if it were free of charge.

◉ When tariffs were removed on television sets, the U.S. television industry was destroyed by cheap imports. Doesn't it follow that removing tariffs on all commodities would destroy all U.S. industry?

◬ The argument is totally wrong. Some U.S. industries are inefficient compared to foreign industries. These industries would be harmed, and possibly forced into bankruptcy, with serious import competition. However, other U.S. industries not only survive but also thrive when tariffs are removed mutually by the United States and its trading partners. These are efficient industries. Expanding production in efficient industries and getting rid of inefficient industries adds to economic efficiency (economists call that "specializing in efficient industries"). Also, removal of tariffs makes prices to consumers go down and the variety and quality of goods and services go up, as long as imports increase. It is true that the owners of inefficient industries and workers in the industries are harmed by tariff removal—these people would suffer, but they are the only people hurt.

Improvements in economic efficiency are by definition good for the overall economy and also are good for many people, but rarely are good for everyone. Unfortunate, but a fact of economic life and possibly of life itself! Any change, no matter how good for the overall economy and overall society, usually hurts *some* people. For example, the shift to the word processor and then to the personal computer brought tremendous benefits to consumers and businesses. We don't stop to consider that, in the process, it destroyed the livelihoods of typewriter manufacturers and workers in that industry, as well as that of typewriter repairpersons.

◉ How are currency exchange rates determined? Is there some central body that decides it on a daily basis, or is it just the reported average of what traders are doing on any given day?

◬ An exchange rate is the price of one currency in terms of another currency. For example, the yen/dollar exchange is the number of yen per dollar. Normally, the exchange rate is determined by demand and supply. U.S. exports of goods and services to Japan, and Japanese investment in the United States, give rise either to a demand for dollars or a supply of yen. Japanese need dollars to pay for the U.S. stuff, or Americans get yen in payment and want dollars. U.S. imports of goods and services, and Americans investing in Japan, mean a supply of dollars or demand for yen. Americans need yen to pay for the Japanese stuff, or Japanese get dollars and want their own currency.

The higher the demand for yen (supply of dollars), the more "unfavorable" the exchange rate for Americans (that is, it takes less yen to buy a dollar, or more dollars to buy a yen). The higher the supply of yen (demand for dollars), the more "favorable" the exchange rate (it takes more yen to buy a dollar, or less dollars to buy a yen). So the exchange rate increasing (for example, from 200 to 225 yen per dollar) means that the dollar is worth more in terms of the yen.

The normal, and ideal, situation is for the exchange rate to "float freely" in the foreign-exchange market. Because there are so many buyers and sellers of foreign exchange, competition results in a free-market price for the exchange rate.

However, either or both of the countries' central banks (the Federal Reserve and the Bank of Japan) could decide not to let the free foreign-exchange market work. At the extreme, the central bank could fix the exchange rate at a certain level (for example, 150 yen per dollar) and keep it there. That is called an exchange-rate peg. Or, the central bank could keep the exchange rate within a certain range (for example, between 125 and 175 yen) and let it move freely only within that range. Also, the central bank could smooth the exchange rate (by buying or selling yen for dollars) within the range, or even if there is no range.

The actual reported exchange rate typically refers to transactions between New York banks at noon in a trading day. There is a variable spread between the selling and buying rates of dealers. The spread is widest at the foreign-exchange shops at airports. Therefore that is the

home than abroad means more foreign funds would be invested in the country. There would be a greater foreign demand for the domestic currency to purchase securities, and again the country's currency increases in value.

Expectations are also important. If it is generally believed that policy making in the country will be irresponsible (examples include the government printing money like mad or confiscating businesses), then that country's currency may fall in value even before these policies are carried out! Why? Because individuals and businesses are rational. They behave on the basis of all available information, even if that information is about the future rather than the present.

Why would the U.S. government ever want a weak dollar?

A weak dollar means an unusually low exchange value of the dollar: For example, 80 yen per dollar, when the exchange rate was formerly 120 yen per dollar. This means that it takes 33 percent less yen than at the earlier exchange rate to get a dollar. So American goods and services cost the Japanese much less yen than at the earlier exchange rate. Obviously, this would cause an increase of exports of American goods and services to Japan. By the same argument, at the new exchange rate it takes $\frac{1}{80}$ of a dollar to buy a yen, whereas previously the yen was $\frac{1}{120}$ dollar. So it takes 50 percent more dollars to buy a yen than at the previous exchange rate. As a consequence, Japanese goods and services would be much more expensive for Americans, which would reduce American imports of goods and services from Japan.

It is reasonable to assume that the low exchange value of the dollar applies not only to the yen but also to currencies of the most important trading partners of the United States. Then, generally, the weak dollar enhances the competitiveness of American business. U.S. commodities are cheaper compared to foreign commodities, both at home and abroad. U.S. exports increase and imports decrease. The result is a reduced deficit on goods and services, which increases output (GDP) and expands employment, in order to produce the higher output.

Another advantage of the weaker dollar is that it means a smaller increase, or even a decrease, in the debt that U.S. residents owe to foreigners. There is a long-term consequence of a deficit on goods and services not compensated by a high-enough surplus on income (interest and dividend and employee-compensation receipts exceeding payments) and on unilateral transfers (more gifts and aid coming in from foreigners than going out). The deficit adds to U.S. debt to foreigners. In effect, foreigners are lending the United States money to finance the U.S. deficit on goods and services, income, and unilateral transfers. Debt has to be paid back, with interest.

So the way to reduce the U.S. foreign debt is to have a surplus on goods and services, income, and unilateral transfers. A sufficiently weak dollar would bring about a surplus on goods and services, and likely also a surplus taking account of income and unilateral transfers.

However, there are disadvantages to a weaker dollar. First, it makes U.S. real and financial assets (such as businesses, and stocks and bonds) cheaper for foreigners, and so U.S. debt to foreigners might actually increase. But that would happen only if foreigners believe that the asset prices are only temporarily cheap. If they think that the low prices are more or less permanent, or as likely to fall as to rise in the future, then the low prices will not induce them to buy U.S. assets. They would not be able to make a profit by reselling the assets in the future.

Second, the weaker dollar reduces the standard of living of U.S. residents as a group. Imported goods and services, and the commodities made from them, are all more expensive, and fewer commodities are imported as a consequence. That is not all bad, because it brings Americans closer to living within their means. Foreigners financing the United States enjoying more goods and services that the United States produces cannot go on forever. A weaker dollar begins the inevitable process of living within our means, meaning that ultimately the dollar total of our exports of goods of services, receipts from income (interest, dividends, and employee compensation), and gifts received is no longer below the dollar total of our imports, payments of income, and donations.

◎ What is the International Monetary Fund, and what does it do?

Ⓐ The International Monetary Fund, commonly referred to as "the IMF" or "the Fund," is an international organization concerned with monetary relations among countries. This means that it exercises monitoring (called "surveillance") over exchange rates of countries and also reviews their monetary and fiscal policies. You can say that the global financing system is the responsibility of the Fund, but the Fund is not an agency of a world government—because there is no world government. So all that the Fund can do is make recommendations to its member countries, rather than issue orders to them.

There is an exception. As you might suspect from its full name, the Fund has control of a fund of currencies. The currencies are provided by member countries to the Fund when they join and periodically thereafter. The Fund lends out these currencies to countries that need them to finance their balance-of-payments deficits. An international currency, called "Special Drawing Rights" (SDRs), is also involved in these lending arrangements. Countries contribute currencies to the Fund and receive borrowing rights to the currencies in proportion to Fund measure of the countries' economic size, which is altered periodically over time.

Voting rights in the Fund are also in proportion to the Fund's measure of economic size. What this means is that the Fund is run by the big powers, especially the United States, the United Kingdom, Europe (the EU countries), Japan, and China. Formally, the Fund is run by international civil servants. In actuality, everyone is aware that the big powers have effective control, if only in the background.

Only a portion of borrowing rights is automatic. Most borrowing requires permission from the Fund, and that means permission from those countries that, in essence, run the Fund. So countries in the big-power group or those aligned with these countries tend to receive loans more readily than small, unaligned, developing countries. The latter countries generally have their borrowing requests examined with thoroughness and must commit to follow strict conditions for receiving loans. In fact, the Fund's language involves the term "conditionality" in that context.

The Fund has many economists working for it, and they do good economic research, which the Fund publishes. The Fund also assembles lots of good economic data for its member countries and for the world economy. You can get the data on the Fund's Web site, but—to the dismay of those doing economic research—you have to pay for the best stuff.

Q What is the difference between the International Monetary Fund and the World Bank?

A The World Bank is concerned with helping developing countries. The International Monetary Fund is oriented to the international financial system. So the Bank makes loans only to developing countries, while the Fund lends to both developed and developing countries.

The Fund obtains its monies from member country "subscriptions" according to the country's economic size, as determined by the Fund. The World Bank obtains most of its funds by borrowing—and it has a great credit rating. So the Bank pays a low interest rate and lends the funds out at favorable terms to the developing countries. Funds to help the poorest countries are obtained largely from donations from richer countries, and the poorest countries receive grants in addition to loans, the latter on very favorable terms.

It is a fair statement that, unless you are a middle-income developing country or a poor country, the Fund is much more important to you than is the Bank.

Q Since the world economy seems so connected, should there be a global economic watchdog that could intervene when, for example, Chinese or U.S.

economic wrongdoing affects the economy of Germany, Nigeria, or Singapore?

A There are some international organizations that do, or could do, something like what you suggest—but only in a limited way. The United Nations (UN), especially its Security Council, is a body concerned with peaceful and cooperative relations among countries. Countries can complain to the UN when they believe that they have been wronged by other countries. However, the UN is effective only when the big powers want it to be. If the big powers—especially the five permanent members of the Security Council (the United States, United Kingdom, France, Russia, and China), who have veto power—do not agree on substantive action to resolve a complaint, then the UN will do nothing substantive.

Another international organization is the International Monetary Fund (IMF). The IMF is supposed to monitor the exchange rate and macroeconomic policy of member countries. In principle, that includes the ramifications of the exchange rate or macroeconomic policy of one country on the economic well-being of another country. In practice, that does not happen.

For example, a country could manage the exchange value of its currency so that it has a competitive advantage in trade. The fewer U.S. dollars it takes to buy one Chinese yuan (the more yuan it takes to buy a dollar), the cheaper Chinese exports are to Americans and the more expensive American exports are to Chinese. So, in keeping its currency low in value relative to the dollar, China encourages its exports to the United States and discourages its imports from the United States. That worsens the U.S. trade deficit with China. Even if the United States were to complain to the IMF about the undervaluation of the yuan, it is not clear that the IMF could take action under its rules and unlikely that it would even express an opinion on the matter.

It is true that when the IMF makes loans to other countries, it can set conditions that include alterations in the country's exchange rate and macroeconomic policies. However, these conditions concern the economic well-being of the borrowing country alone. They have no relationship to the effects of that country's policies on the economic well-being of other countries.

The World Trade Organization (WTO) is more geared to what you suggest. The WTO is set up to receive and resolve complaints about violations of trade agreements, such as imposing discriminatory tariffs on a member country or instituting quotas limiting the amount of imports of particular commodities from a member country. However, the WTO has no means of enforcing its rulings. A country found in violation of a WTO rule or a WTO trade agreement can refuse to make the necessary correction (for example, removing the discriminatory tariff or the quota). At that point, the WTO encourages the complaining country and the country in violation to negotiate a settlement.

Failing that, the complaining country is permitted to retaliate against the country found in violation, for example, by imposing its own discriminatory tariff or quota against important exports of the country found in violation. Really, all that the WTO does regarding complaints by one country against another is to provide a convenient forum whereby the countries involved can do what they probably would do if there were no WTO!

To sum up, the world is far from having a "global economic watchdog." An effective watchdog would probably require a world government behind it—and we are far from having that as well. You ask, though, not whether we have a global economic watchdog, but whether having one would be a good idea. The answer is not necessarily "yes." Not all economic decisions of national governments are sensible. Sometimes such decisions go against the market system and reduce economic efficiency. It is not obvious that a global economic watchdog would behave differently from national governments in this respect.

Q What's after globalization?

A Globalization means a number of things. The first is freer international trade in goods and services. The second is freer movement of capital across countries. Logically, along with capital, there should be freer migration of people, especially workers, from one country to another. That has not happened; but the march of globalization in other respects has not been slowed. The third is freer transfer of technology between countries. The fourth is the spread of capitalism and the market system to countries previously only marginally in the international trading system: Russia, other ex-Soviet Union countries, Eastern European countries, China, and—to a lesser but vitally important extent—India. The fifth is the incorporation of these countries into the international economy.

The sixth meaning of globalization is the tremendous increase in domestic companies importing parts for their products from abroad and/or assembling products abroad, and/or servicing products abroad. If the foreign firm doing these things is legally part of the domestic company (a subsidiary or affiliate firm), then the transfer of work abroad is called "offshoring." If the foreign firm is legally unrelated to the domestic firm, then the transfer of work is termed "outsourcing." Of course, offshoring and outsourcing have their domestic counterparts. An entirely domestic vertically integrated firm (that is, a business producing its own parts for its salable product, assembling the product itself, and having its own marketing, legal, and accounting departments) corresponds to an offshoring situation.

The phenomenon of "contracting out" is the domestic equivalent of outsourcing. I have a friend who owned a carpet retailing company. He also was the only worker for the company. His business physical assets (capital) consisted of a telephone (there were no cell phones at the time), a van, and many books of sample carpets. When a sale was made, he contracted out the carpet manufacture and the carpet installation. Then he drove to the next prospective customer and, if there was a sale, repeated the procedure.

Will globalization ever end? One realistic possibility is that the process of increases in the six phenomena mentioned above comes to a halt: globalization stops. That would mean the end of globalization defined as increases in the phenomena, but it would not mean a reverse of the globalization that has occurred to date. Even if globalization reverses itself, as long as the reversal is small, the fact of globalization remains.

One way for globalization truly to end would be politically successful protectionist movements in countries crucial to the functioning of a global economy. First and foremost among these countries is the United States. Others are the United Kingdom, the European Union (EU), Canada, Switzerland, and Japan. These are the main industrial countries of the world (allowing that the EU consists of a group of such countries). It is conceivable that some of these countries could withdraw, even partially, from the international global economy by systematically ceasing to honor obligations under the World Trade Organization (WTO) or by systematically taking advantage of loopholes in the rules of the WTO. The damage to the global economy would be devastating.

The outcome of this withdrawal would be high tariffs and high nontrade barriers (such as quotas and administrative hassles for imports) and restrictions on capital flows and technology transfers—beginning with the countries that began the process and then spreading throughout the world. As a result, the shift of Russia, China, and India to capitalism and the market system could be reversed, as the governments of these countries might try to preserve their economic growth by returning to their previous economic system.

Why would this process of disintegration of the global economy begin? Because some industries and labor groups in the industrial countries are harmed by globalization. Freer trade in goods and services in general, especially in the form of offshoring and outsourcing, takes business away from domestic firms and jobs away from domestic labor. It is true that other domestic firms gain business and profits, and other labor groups in the domestic economy experience more jobs and higher wages. Also, the economy as a whole gains, as economic efficiency is enhanced by globalization. However, the conspicuous nature of the business and labor groups harmed by globalization could intersect with their political influence. A switch from globalization to protectionism could result.

An alternative way for globalization to end could be through regionalism. Even under globalization, regional groups—exemplified by the EU and North American Free Trade Agreement (NAFTA), and various similar organizations among developing countries—have increased in number. The EU is an example of a customs union under which member countries remove all barriers to the movement of goods, services, capital, and people among themselves. That seems like globalization; but it is only "regionalism" (the word "regionalization" is not used). The customs union erects a common trade policy—common tariffs and nontrade barriers—against imports from the outside world. Also, the free movement of people does not apply except within the customs union.

A free-trade area such as NAFTA involves member countries having mutual free trade in goods and services only. The members retain their own trade restrictions against other countries. Also, there is no free movement of people, or even of workers, among member countries. A free-trade area is also regionalism, though in a partial sense compared to a customs union.

The important point is that, under either form of regionalism, imports of goods and services from the rest of the world are subject to discriminatory treatment. Free trade in goods and services—and even free movement of people—among a limited group of countries is not necessarily a move toward globalization.

Will there be a post-globalization era? If so, what form will it take? I do not know. But one way to help prevent globalization from ending would be for governments to take steps to have a "safety net" for workers who lose jobs due to globalization. Ideally, this would take the form of retraining away from jobs in industries that globalization harms and toward jobs in industries producing for the global economy. That policy in itself would help make the economy more efficient and enhance economic growth.

In contrast, I personally do not advocate aid ("bailouts") for firms that lose customers, revenue, and profits because they cannot compete in the global economy—or indeed for any other reason. It is up to management, and stockholders, to have the foresight to switch the firm to efficient production of goods in demand in the global economy, and otherwise to sell off the firm's assets or merge with another firm. If none of these events happen and the firm goes bankrupt or is taken over by another firm, it is deservedly—at least from the standpoint of economic efficiency.

ADDITIONAL RESOURCES

The following lists of additional resources are offered to broaden and deepen the "refined common sense" that is the hallmark of *Everyday Economics*. While the recommended resources are biased by my own preferences, I invite the reader to consult the Web site http://www.rfe.org, which provides systematic referencing (and easy linking) of a much larger set of online resources with an economics orientation. This is the "Resources for Economists" Web site, sponsored by the American Economic Association. The resources in this section are handpicked for their usefulness and include print as well as online material.

1. Encyclopedias

Three encyclopedias published by Palgrave Macmillan were my primary resource for the research underlying the writing of *Everyday Economics*. In my opinion, these encyclopedias are the best sources for background information on common-sense economics. Each encyclopedia has many entries, authored by experts in particular fields. Note that although these publications are called "dictionaries," they are really encyclopedias.

The New Palgrave Dictionary of Economics, second edition, edited by Steven N. Durlauf and Lawrence E. Blume, is the most recent, and most relevant, of these encyclopedias. The print edition consists of eight volumes, and every branch of economics and virtually every economic issue is covered. This encyclopedia has the additional advantage of an online edition, located at http://www.dictionaryofeconomics.com/dictionary. You have to subscribe to the online edition, but "teasers" are provided free.

The New Palgrave Dictionary of Money and Finance, edited by Peter Newman, Murray Milgate, and John Eatwell, has three volumes and specializes in money, banking, and finance.

The New Palgrave Dictionary of Economics and the Law, edited by Peter Newman, also consists of three volumes, and is even more specialized.

By Googling "economics online encyclopedias," one can access a variety of economics encyclopedias and dictionaries. A focused list of dictionaries, glossaries and encyclopedias for economics and business is in http://www.rfe.org/showCat.php?cat_id=10. The online encyclopedias that I like best are the following:

Encyclopedia of Economic and Business History, http://eh.net/encyclopedia, is oriented to laypersons and students. It has a historical focus.

The Concise Encyclopedia of Economics, http://www.econlib.org/library/CEE.html, has very brief entries, but is good for an overview of a topic.

Economicae: An Illustrated Encyclopedia of Economics, http://www.unc.edu/depts/econ/byrns_web/Economicae/EconomicaeA.htm, has a neat interactive format. It is intermediate between an encyclopedia and a glossary.

Wikipedia, http://www.wikipedia.org, is a special kind of encyclopedia. I consult Wikipedia for insight to how people think about issues rather than for information on the issues themselves.

2. Glossaries

Federal Reserve Bank of San Francisco Glossary of Economic Terms, http://www.frbsf.org/tools/glossary/index.html, has very short entries, but that is how a glossary is supposed to present information.

Accounting, Business Studies and Economics Dictionary, http://www.tuition.com.hk/dictionary, provides short definitions of terms.

Personal Finance Glossary, http://www.mortgageloan.com/finance-glossary, is oriented to personal finance defined narrowly but haphazardly. It is weird that there is no entry for "hedge funds."

The Glossary at Measuring Worth, http://www.measuringworth.com/glossary/index.html, is specific to the calculators and data sets of that Web site. The calculators measure economic worth over time. (Disclosure: I am co-founder and Director of Research of Measuring Worth.)

3. Textbooks

There are a large number of introductory economics textbooks available, and more seem to be produced every year. There is not much difference among the textbooks, but, as a teacher of introductory economics for almost four decades, I have found that two textbooks are a cut above the rest, and I am currently using them in my introductory economics classes at University of Illinois at Chicago. These textbooks, like most introductory texts, are available also in split form, Microeconomics and Macroeconomics separately.

Paul Krugman and Robin Wells, *Economics* (Worth Publishers) is the first textbook recommended. Krugman is a Nobel Laureate whose economics views, whether at an introductory or advanced level, are always worth reading. The interesting thing about the Krugman-Wells textbook is that economics is presented objectively, with the ideological (liberal) orientation of Krugman rarely apparent. I find that the second edition of this text marks a significant improvement over the initial edition.

James D. Gwartney, Richard L. Stroup, Russel S. Sobel, and David A. Macpherson, *Economics: Private and Public Choice* (South-Western Cengage) has gone through twelve editions. Its orientation is slightly more toward business than is Krugman and Wells, if only because of the attention given to entrepreneurship.

4. Government Web Sites

For factual information, all sorts of statistics, and consumer advice, I recommend Googling U.S. federal government websites at http://www.google.com/unclesam. Especially valuable are the following sites:

Federal Trade Commission, http://www.ftc.gov, provides consumer information.

Bureau of Labor Statistics, http://www.bls.gov, is oriented to the workplace (wages, employment, unemployment, productivity, worker injuries, consumer price index).

Census Bureau, http://www.census.gov, has a wealth of data on people, households, and industry.

Board of Governors of the Federal Reserve System, http://www.federalreserve.gov, offers banking information and statistics.

Bureau of Economic Analysis, http://www.bea.gov, is the first place to go for macroeconomic statistics.

5. Blogs

A large number of blogs with economic content is at http://www.rfe.org/showCat.php?cat_id=96. The blogs that I recommend are the following:

The Conscience of a Liberal, http://krugman.blogs.nytimes.com, presents the views of Nobel Laureate Paul Krugman. The blogger is a great economist with a social conscience.

Blogs with a free-market orientation are **The Adam Smith Institute Blog,** http://www.adamsmith.org/blog, and **Econlog,** http://econlog.econlib.org. The latter blog is sponsored by the same people who bring you The Concise Encyclopedia of Economics.

Grasping Reality, http://www.j-bradford-delong.net/movable_type, is an idiosyncratic and provocative blog produced by Brad DeLong.

Businomics Blog, http://businomics.typepad.com, offers the down-to-earth commentary of Bill Conerly.

Marginal Revolution, http://www.marginalrevolution.com, goes far beyond economics in its revelations.

Real Time Economics, http://blogs.wsj.com/economics, is the blog of the *Wall Street Journal,* and comments on current economic events.

6. Economic Reporting

A longer list is in http://www.rfe.org/showCat.php?cat_id=41, but you can't go wrong with the following sites:

Bloomberg.com, http://www.bloomberg.com/news/economy, is the only recommended site not based on a newspaper or magazine.

Economic-oriented Web sites emanating from media with a long print history are:

The Economist, http://www.economist.com/finance
New York Times, http://topics.nytimes.com/top/reference/timestopics/subjects/e/economic_conditions_and_trends/index.html
Washington Post, http://www.washingtonpost.com/wp-dyn/content/business/economy/index.html
Wall Street Journal, http://online.wsj.com/public/page/news-business-us.html
I also recommend *TIME,* http://www.time.com/time/business.